Published under the aegis of

Center for Communication and Information Sciences

(Victoria University; University of Toronto at Mississauga;
University of Helsinki; Universidad Sao Paulo, Brasil; Indiana University;
University of Lugano; University of Ottawa)

Series: *Language, Media & Education Studies*

Edited by: Marcel Danesi & Leonard G. Sbrocchi

1. M. Danesi, *Interpreting Advertisements. A Semiotic Guide*
2. M. Angenot, *Critique of Semiotic Reason*
3. S. Feigenbaum, *The Intermediate Sign in the System of French and Hebrew Verbs*
4. A. Bailin, *Metaphor and the Logic of Language Use*
5. C. D. E. Tolton, ed., *The Cinema of Jean Cocteau*
6. C. Madott Kosnik, *Primary Education: Goals, Processes and Practices*
7. F. Nuessel, *The Esperanto Language*
8. M. G. Guido, *The Acting Reader*
9. F. Ratto, *Hobbes tra scienza della politica e teoria delle passioni*
10. S. Battestini, *African Writing and Text*
11. T. A. Sebeok, *Essays in Semiotics I: Life Signs*
12. T. A. Sebeok, *Essays in Semiotics II: Culture Signs*
13. A. Ponzio and S. Petrilli, *Philosophy of Language, Art and Answerability in Mikhail Bakhtin*
14. R. Beasley, M. Danesi, P. Perron, *Signs for Sale. An Outline of Semiotic Analysis for Advertisers & Marketers*
15. F. Merrell, *Signs for Everybody, or, Chaos, Quandaries and Communication*
16. P. Perron, L.G. Sbrocchi, P. Colilli, M. Danesi (eds.) *Semiotics as a Bridge between the Humanities and the Sciences*
17. A. Makolkin, *Anatomy of Heroism*
18. P. Perron, M. Danesi, J. Umiker-Sebeok, A. Watanabe (eds.) *Semiotics and Information Sciences*
19. T. A. Sebeok, *The Swiss Pioneer in Nonverbal Communication Studies. Heine Hediger (1908-1992)*
20. M. Danesi (ed.), *The Invention of Global Semiotics*
21. T. A. Sebeok, *Semiotic Prologues*
22. R. Dalvesco, *Fuller Speak*
23. F. Merrell, *Learning Living, Living Learning: Signs Between East and West*
24. J. Kelly (ed.), *Looking Up; Science and Observation in the Early Modern Period*

Cover: *Semiotics as venture of the future.* Compugraphics by P. Bertrand

John Deely

SEMIOTICS SEEN SYNCHRONICALLY: THE VIEW FROM 2010

LEGAS

New York   Ottawa   Toronto

3

Library and Archives Canada Cataloguing in Publication

Deely, John N.
    Semiotics seen synchronically : the view
from 2010 / John Deely.

(Language, media & education studies ; 47)
Includes bibliographical references and index.
ISBN 978-1-897493-17-5

    1. Semiotics. I. Title. II. Series: Language, media
& education studies ; 47.

P99.D427 2010   302.2   C2010-901206-2

Cover symbol
In the early days of the Semiotic Society of America, Brooke Williams Deely pointed out to me that "the caduceus, the staff of a messenger bearing a message, is *a sign of a sign*". The cover illustration combines this symbol to illustrate the "venture of the future" that semiotics represents for the intellectual culture of any time.

http://www.legaspublishing.com

LEGAS
P. O. Box 040328   3 Wood Aster Bay   5201 Dufferin Street
Brooklyn, New York   Ottawa, Ontario   Toronto, Ontario
USA 11204   K2R 1B3   M3H 5T8

Printed and bound in Canada by Gauvin Press

This work is dedicated

to the semioticians of the 22nd century

Contents

SEMIOTICS SEEN SYNCHRONICALLY:
THE VIEW FROM 2010

Preface

"... since the life of signs does not stop, of course,
with their fixation into objects. ... existential signs ...
are always in a state of becoming. ... pause is always temporary."
— *Eero Tarasti 2000: 7*

This little book is a development, originally for an article at the request of Jiazu ("Charles") Gu as Editor of *Chinese Semiotic Studies*, of my formal remarks on the semiotic heritage delivered on Wednesday, 23 September 2009, as Chair of the Mesa Redonda/Round Table "La Tradition Semiòtica/Semiotics Heritage", participated in by Solomon Marcus (Romania), Vilmos Voigt (Hungary), José Romera Castillo (Spain), and Chie Sou Kim (Korea), in the framework of the 22–26 September 10th World Congress of the International Association for Semiotic Studies held in the city of A Coruña, Galicia, Spain, at the Faculty of Sociology and Law of the University of A Coruña, Campus Elviña.

The work develops over four chapters.

Chapter 1 will be an outline of the framework within which I will principally consider semiotic development.

Chapter 2 will present an overview of the semiotic development as it has occurred within the synchronic framework established in Chapter 1, as that framework nears the inevitable "diachronic turn" where the present author ceases to belong to the living population, which alone defines the non-geometrical reality of "synchrony" as an open-ended 'new beginning' which, perforce, will occupy subsequently and diachronically its own "slice of time".

Chapter 3 will present an analysis in detail of what we have learned—in this transitional synchronic phase (as pointed out shortly below by Petrilli) that we call "semiotics" today—that is of theoretical import for the "doctrine" or (cenoscopic) "science" of signs as it implies and establishes a definitively postmodern and global intellectual culture revealing the inherent possibilities of semiosis as mastered within semiotics to provide the cenoscopic antidote (both transdisciplinary and interdisciplinary) to the intense specialization which alone made possible the ideoscopic development of science in the modern sense—an original "synchrony" in its own right in the overlapping lifetimes of Galileo, Poinsot, and Descartes.

Chapter 4, the brief conclusion, will be a "parting summation" (intended especially to finalize the most fundamental sense of "synchronicity" introduced within and applied throughout this essay).

Chapter 1

Outline of the Framework

1.1. Standpoint of the Essay

We come from the womb, each of us, with no experience of the "external world" (as the modern philosophers called our surroundings), so it is not surprising that we all begin with a synchronic view that takes no account of history. A first-time visitor to Beijing in 2004 went on a sight-seeing walk with two colleagues, both of whom had been to Beijing previously, but not for some time. The two kept uttering marveling comments on the changes in the city, till finally their exasperated first-time visitor companion said emphatically: "I don't see any changes at all."

Henri Bergson (1859–1941) called it (1907) "the natural geometry of the human intellect", to wit, the tendency to see everything in terms of the individual's "here and now", as if the present were eternal.

Experience early on forces at least some minimal awareness of a difference between past and present, and of future possibilities not all of which are predictable on the basis of either past or present. But to this historical dimension of human awareness there is a resistance, and only gradually do human animals (as distinguished from other animals) begin to take serious account of a past without which their present would not be at all, or of a future which offers unpredictable possibilities as well as mere extensions of the past. And *only* human animals, precisely through metasemiosis,[1] are able to become aware of

---

[1]"Metasemiosis" consists in the awareness which the human animal, in using signs as every animal must, achieves with the intellectual realization that the being proper to signs consists in triadic relations, invisible as relations to sense perception, transcending every subjective boundary, and upon which every achievement of human knowledge depends. This is the realization identifying the human being, in order to be a "rational animal" (animal rationale) or "thinking thing" (or res cogitans), as having to be, yet more fundamentally and integrally, a semiotic animal, the only such animal on earth, with the responsibility that imposes—semioethics, as we will have occasion below to mention. On this term (and on the oxymoronic internal contradictoriness—the simple illegitimacy—of the linguistic expression "metasemiotics"), see Deely 2009b: iii–iv, xiv, 127, 194, 198, 199. (Of course, one can always try, Humpty-Dumpty style ["Words mean what I want them to mean; no more and no less"—see note 38 of Chapter 3, p. 70 below], to stipulate a meaning for 'metasemiotics' that overcomes the historicity of its oxymoronic baggage; but the arbitrariness of stipulation seldom trumps historicity [see Deely 2009c:

a past preceding their own synchronicity yet entering into and influencing that very synchronicity in ways that elude full consciousness even while shaping present consciousness and passing through it "diachronically" by extending the synchronicity of a given life into the larger synchronicity of the species as a whole[2] in the universe of which it is a part.

This is the passage from the partial illusion of synchrony to the full reality of diachrony, and both perspectives are essential to the maturation of human understanding; for the present, even though it has no stationary point (inasmuch as each present moment is the simultaneous becoming of past and future), yet is the whole of the "land of the living", into which enter and out of which exit new individuals, so that the population neither is nor can be wholly constant, determined, once and for all. This side of the grave, for the human animals, there neither is nor can be a "once and for all" synchrony; before conception and birth is too early, after death is too late, and during life the perspective on the external surroundings as it opened at birth is constantly deepening in spite of all,[3] as our "glassy essence" becomes a veritable "bottomless lake" as we ourselves exit that "land of the living" which, at any given moment, constitutes the "present" population of human animals.

When I speak, then, of "synchrony" in this essay, I do not mean synchrony in the geometric sense of a timeless abstraction horizontally slicing across human experience for all time, as if with no vertical dimension actual or possible,[4] but rather in the actual or "temporal" sense according to which the present population of living human ani-

---

Chap. 6], and what really would be the gain of success, anyway, in this case, even should it be achieved?) really would be the gain of success, anyway, in this case, even should it be achieved?)

[2] It is the whole problem of a "collective unconscious", of the Heideggerean "House of Being". See Deely 2000, and 2005.

[3] Deely 1992a.

[4] It was in this geometrical sense of synchrony, as we will see, that Saussure (1857–1913) conceived the matter in his original "signifiant/signifié" model proposed for semiotic development in the early 20th century. Jakobson (1896–1982) , more than Lotman (1922–1993), in taking up Saussure's model, yet qualified its "arbitrariness" sufficiently to leave an opening from Saussure's own "geometrical synchronicity" to the actuality of "temporal synchronicity" which I employ in this essay. Actual synchronicity, taken as beginning at any definite "present moment" (e.g., AD1916), from that moment begins to "expand" by constituting a definite temporal cross-section within the cultural and intellectual consciousness of a given community — in this case, the "community of inquirers" focused on the matter of signs at work in the world within and around us. The fact that such a community, as a community among the living, definitely formed in the 20th century, as Petrilli remarks (2008: 3), is the synchronic view I want to present in these pages.

mals has developed within itself—in contrast to relatively isolated individuals here and there wondering about signs and their role—a veritable "community of inquirers", species-specifically human, which takes the action of signs as its focus and—expanding at first mainly horizontally (synchronically) but (inevitably), with the passage of time, vertically (diachronically) as well, especially as living members pass away and new individuals enter the discourse.

It was in this sense of synchronicity, for example, that Susan Petrilli delivered her Sebeok Fellow Address to the Semiotic Society of America on 17 October 2008 (a Thursday, as it happened) on the occasion of the SSA's 33rd Annual Meeting in Houston, Texas, USA:[5]

> In these remarks I want to look at semiotics, as it were, more synchronically than diachronically. It is not the whole history of semiotic development as a consciousness of the fundamental role of signs in life and experience that I want to discuss, but rather the contemporary phenomenon that we today who have lived in both the 20th and the 21st century have witnessed and participated in as the development of *semiotics*. For though there is of course a long history behind the semiotics of today, still there is a sense in which semiotics is, as a widespread intellectual movement, a phenomenon more "of our time" than it is of any time past. So it is mainly of figures alive in the 20th century, and a few of them still alive today, that I want to speak.

So too my focus in this essay is synchronic in the expanding or temporal sense explained above, especially since I have already set out, in my *Four Ages of Understanding* volume,[6] a "whole history of semiotic development" insofar as such an exposition pertains to philosophy as the basic cenoscopic science. My focus in the present work is on "the sense in which semiotics is, as a widespread intellectual movement, a phenomenon more 'of our time' than it is of any time past", however much into the future it will perdure.

1.2. Synchrony's Inevitable Seepage into Diachrony: the Historicity of Human Use of Signs

Yet, indeed, the past is closing in upon us; so much so that we, who are still living members of the societies of human animals who first engendered a "community of inquirers" focused on the action of signs, must already look to the 20th century "founding figures", even among those whom we personally knew and with whom we worked, as no longer

---

[5] Petrilli 2008: 3.

[6] Deely 2001, subtitled The first postmodern survey of philosophy from ancient times to the turn of the 21st century (Toronto, Canada: University of Toronto Press).

living. From them we may still learn, indeed (that is the miraculous aspect of diachrony), but no longer they from us (the main limit of synchrony as intersecting diachrony). We ourselves, indeed, approach that "far boundary" where the community of living inquirers, the "temporally synchronic" investigators of the sign, will no longer include us but only—if anything—our works within its boundaries. At that frontier, in short, we may or may not continue diachronically to influence the future of semiotic development, depending on the fate among the living of our recordings in whatever media; but we will no longer be ourselves subjectively existing and adding "new materials" to the heritage of which we shall have (at that point) become "past part".

So our "boundary of time" yields our definition of synchrony in terms of those with whom we can intersubjectively have intellectual exchange, in contrast with the bare suprasubjectivity[7] of those whose lifetime does not overlap our own, from whom we can indeed *learn* but without the possibility of *their learning* from us, from what we have learned in turn. So synchrony as a temporal reality is a one-way movement into a limited future, in contrast with diachrony which not only arises from within synchrony but also invades it from a past before the synchrony in question began in the first place, and extends beyond that synchrony into a future accessible only to those who "come after" into the "land of the living."[8] As far as concerns the formation of a "community of inquirers", then, beyond the central matter of a "shared focus", the already dead define the past; the not yet living define the future; the not yet dead define *the present, the "synchronicity"* within which we are influenced by others (living or dead) but can influence directly (through dyadic interactions presupposed to Thirdness) only those around us; but beyond them also (through Thirdness alone) can we influence some at least of those to come "after us", i.e., after we no longer exist subjectively involved in interactions and intersubjectivity, though suprasubjectively, through semiosis, we may indeed continue "objectively" in the indirect influences of pure relativity shaping the future in normally unpredictable ways.

From the standpoint of the present, when did "semiotics" begin? The answer already takes us beyond synchronicity, yet not all that far (backward) from the land of the living, if we distinguish the *actual formation* of a community of inquirers properly called "semioticians" from the *nominalist question* of the coinage of the term "semiotics". The nominalist question, interestingly enough, already involves us in a diachrony whereby the past invades the serious formation of "semioticians" as the phenomenon of a coalescence of 20th century inquirers into

---

[7] See "Why Intersubjectivity Is Not Enough", Chap. 9 in Deely 2009c.
[8] See "The Boundary of Time", Preface to Deely 2001: xix–xxxiii.

a community investigating signs and the action of signs. The "invasion", on this nominalist point, however, does not pass through the work of Saussure, the first actual figure around whom this community began its coalescence, but directly through Lotman who, as a follower of Saussure in the matter of the model proposed under the name of "semiology", yet departed from Saussure in his choice of name for the new science by reason of a more informed historicity.

Let us, then, treat the two questions—nominalistic, on the one hand, formative, on the other hand—in turn.

1.3. *The Nominalist Question*

The term "semiotics" comes to us[9] from a grammatically incorrect coinage by John Locke (1632–1704) in 1690 (December of 1689, to be technical), via a never-expressed Latin derivative *semiotica*, to the present usage of "semiotics" to name "the science"—as Ferdinand de Saussure (1857–1913) put it somewhere early in the interval between 1906 and 1911[10]—that "does not yet exist", yet "has a right to existence, a place staked out in advance".

There had been previous discussions of this "science with a right to existence", most especially in 16th and early 17th century Spain[11] and Portugal.[12] The Latins had discussed the question of a (cenoscopic) "science of signs" under the moniker *doctrina signorum*, a usage which goes back at least as far as Augustine of Hippo (AD354–430).[13] Though neither Locke nor Saussure evinced any least awareness of this earlier Latin development—what we now recognize to have been the original or "first" florescence of semiotic consciousness[14]—Locke at least equivalated his coinage as "Σημίωτική or *the Doctrine of Signs*", in this way, albeit unconsciously, establishing a linkage between his own proposal and the earlier Latin discussion—a discussion not only neglected in

---

[9] This is a summary statement of extensive researches into the etymology of all the terminology that has been used in connection with the naming of the study of signs: in particular, besides the references listed in note 19 below, see Deely 2003a, esp. 2004, and 2006b.

[10] Saussure 1916 (= i.1906–1911): 16. But see the detail in note 19 below.

[11] Where Poinsot's culminating *Tractatus* was published in 1632.

[12] Where Poinsot's teachers, the Conimbricenses, had published their commentary *De Signis* in 1606, a work which never appeared outside the Latin language until Doyle's English translation of 2001. This work was a crucial influence on both Peirce and Poinsot (see Beuchot and Deely 1995).

[13] See Deely 2009: *Augustine & Poinsot. The Protosemiotic Development*.

[14] See the "Timeline of Semiotic Development" in Deely 2009: Appendix E, 237–246.

Locke's day[15] but thereafter thoroughly forgotten throughout the whole period of "modern philosophy" as it developed "from Descartes (1596–1650) to Davidson (1917–2003)".

When Thomas A. Sebeok (1920–2001), in 1976, came to write the *Foreword* to his seminal volume *Contributions to the Doctrine of Signs*, he made a major point of choosing this *doctrina signorum* expression for his title, with a twofold objective: first, precisely to align himself with the longer tradition linking through Poinsot "the ancients and the moderns in the history of semiotics";[16] second, to contrast the ceno-scopic nature of semiotics with the ideoscopic approaches which constitute science in the modern sense[17] (and in terms of which Saussure thought exclusively[18]).

Saussure himself, however, knowing neither Locke nor Peirce, Augustine nor Poinsot, the Conimbricenses nor Peirce, simply proposed his own name for this "new science":[19]

---

[15] Ironically, the first systematic treatise fully to establish the semiotic point of view and triadic relation as constituting the formal being of signs, the *Tractatus de Signis* of John Poinsot (1589–1644), was published in the very year of Locke's birth, 1632!

[16] Sebeok 1982: x.

[17] See the biographical account in Williams 2010; and the contrast between the two "semiotic manifestos" of Anderson et al. on one hand and Gardin et al. on the other hand, deliberately published by Sebeok back-to-face in the 1984 volume 52.1 of *Semiotica*. See note 41, p. 38 below.

[18] Cf. Sebeok 1976: ix. Commentary in Deely 1975, 1976, 1977, 1978, 1982a, 1986a.

[19] Saussure 1916: 16. As I noted in Deely 2001: 673, however, Saussure's proposed name for the general study, "semiology", has been traced back (Godel 1957: 275) to November of 1894 in a note definitely from Saussure's own hand; and Naville (1901: 104) reports an earlier version or outline for semiology essentially similar to what will appear in the *Cours* of 1916. Whether Saussure took over the term "semiology", consciously or unconsciously, from some other source or, less probably, conceived it neologistically in his own mind, according to Meier-Oeser (1997: 315) the term has a history of its own among Protestant Latin authors of the late Latin-early modern period. The decisive feature of the proposal so named in Saussure's writing lies in the advice that natural signs are to be treated within semiology, if at all, only through an assimilation to the model of signs as conventional or "arbitrary" (unmotivated by anything in the vehicle's physical structure or subjectivity in their link between sign-vehicle and object-signified).

Had some student of Giambatista Vico (13 June 1668–1744 January 23) entered the discussion of Saussure's day, we might also have had to contend with "sematology" as well as "semiology" in the 20th century settlement upon Locke's "semiotics" as the proper name for the new science (about as helpful as was Tycho Brahe's contribution to the Copernican debate in Galielo's day!). Perhaps just as well such a student did not seriously emerge

I shall call it *semiology* (from the Greek *sēmeîon* 'sign'). Semiology would show what constitutes signs, what laws govern them.

Along with this name, Saussure proposed a model upon which to found or "base" the new science: the linguistic sign understood as providing the "master pattern", *le patron général*, for the whole development. This proposed "foundational model" consisted in a dyadic relation between, basically, the acoustic image of a word heard, called the *signifiant*, as arbitrarily linked with a concept, the mental representation called the *signifié*. And what about the object *other* than the concept, the object presented by the concept? especially when that object is also a physical reality, such as a steak ordered in a restaurant, say, or a mineral inside a mine?

There is no room in Saussure's sign-model for any suprasubjective or intersubjective reality respecting the user of signs, linking those users to the external surroundings of physical things objectified, as we will see; Saussure relegates his proposed "new science" of "semiology" to the realm of "general psychology", even though he demands that this "semiology" be recognized "as an independent science with its own object like all the other sciences."[20] In the beginning, Saussure's *model* proposed (stipulatively, 'arbitrarily', as it were) to be the basis for the new science was accepted unreservedly in East and West alike, but his *name* for the new science was adopted initially only in Western Europe and the Americas. The challenge orchestrated by Sebeok over the 20th century's last four decades to *both* name *and* model came to be the main "story line" in the founding of semiotics as we understand the "doctrine of signs" today.

1.4. The *Actual Formation* of a "Community of Inquirers" Focused on Signs

So far as the work of any single individual inspires the initial coalescence of a *community of inquirers* on the subject of semiotics, it would have to be recognized as the *Cours de linguistique générale* of Ferdinand de Saussure. This work, first published (from materials assembled posthumously by students of Saussure's live classroom presentations) in 1916, provided the original focal point for what became for the first

---

in time, for the complication would not have been particularly helpful, especially when we consider that "sematology" carried much the same linguistic/cultural baggage of (mis)orientation for understanding semiosis that Saussure attached to "semiology". See Eschbach and Trabant, eds. 1983; and Trabant 2004.

[20] Saussure 1916: 16.

time in the 20th century something like a *general interest* across intellectual culture in the subject of signs conceived as "a new science with its own object".

East and West, the study of signs was originally taken up by a whole range of 20th century thinkers who based their work explicitly on Saussure.

In the East, the most seminal of these thinkers was Juri Lotman (1922–1993), father of the "Tartu-Moscow School" of semiotics. Coming to the consideration of signs somewhat later than Saussure and, unlike Saussure, not ignorant of Locke's 1690 proposal that a science of signs be developed under the moniker *semiotics*, Lotman chose to defer to Locke's historical priority in this matter of naming. Thus, even though Lotman embraced Saussure's dyadic *patron général* as an "unrejectable cornerstone" of the science,[21] for the *name* of the new science of signs Lotman adopted from the beginning of his work the name "semiotics" in preference to Saussure's suggestion of "semiology".

East and West, then, the *model basic*—the sign-model taken as foundational—to the developing discussion was the same: Saussure's *signifiant/signifié* dyad. But the developing discussion itself was called "semiology" in the Western intellectual culture, "semiotics" in the Eastern.

Notice that Saussure's model is *stipulated*, or *postulated*, as the basis for the new science. Roughly contemporary with Saussure was a relatively unknown and comparatively neglected figure, the American philosopher-scientist Charles Sanders Peirce (1839–1914), born thus eighteen years earlier but dying only one year earlier than Saussure. Peirce too, but independently, and under some influence of his reading of the later Latins[22] (those who wrote in the centuries immediately before Descartes' advice to his contemporaries to beware of such reading, lest we be unconsciously infected by their errors), came to focus on the idea of semiotics as a possible new "science of signs". Peirce's work in this regard would come to be an influence on Roman Jakobson (1896–1982) and Charles Morris (1901–1979), both of the latter to become teachers of Thomas A. Sebeok (1920–2001). Sebeok, as we shall see, like Saussure a professional linguist, but at the same time also a self-professed "biologist manqué",[23] would prove to be the *pivotal figure* in moving semiotics from the arbitrary foundation laid down by Saussure to the analysis based foundation exemplified by Peirce's work in rejecting a-priori limits for the new science.

With this much preamble, let us sketch first an overview of semi-

---

[21] Lotman 1990, inter alia.
[22] Beuchot and Deely 1995.
[23] See the memorial essay "Thomas A. Sebeok, Biologist Manqué", Deely, 2005a.

otic development today, and then an analysis of the theoretical components or elements essential to the doctrine of signs which establish it as
the positive essence philosophically of a postmodern intellectual culture. Within this culture philosophy as cenoscopic science should
rediscover its proper role (lost since at least the Enlightenment) in providing the means for understanding how the world of culture is not
oppositional to but a species-specifically human extension of the world
of nature—from which the whole of life, nonhuman as well as human,
emerged and upon which all of life depends.

Chapter 2

Overview of the Semiotic Development

The 20th century saw the outburst—for want of a better word—in intellectual culture of an interest in signs. By midpoint this outburst had spread virtually everywhere, and the work of Ferdinand de Saussure was recognized as having been the development's principal inspiration. Yet even so, as noted above, the development proceeded under two different proper names: both as *semiology* in Western Europe and the United States (as Saussure himself had proposed), and as *semiotics* in Eastern Europe (as Locke had first proposed, unknown to Saussure, and as including "ideas", the "formal signs" of the earlier Latins—as well as "words" in the model,[1] a detail which Lotman did not fasten upon, but which, if he had, might have led Soviet Semiotics to the semiotic notion of significate as including, beyond the Saussurean *signifié*, the whole order of physical reality extrasubjectively apprehended as well as 'given').

2.1. The Initial Foundation Proposed in the 20th Century for a New "Science of Signs"

Saussure was a linguist, and also a typically modern intellectual, in that his awareness of philosophical culture was confined to the modern era. He was accordingly (inevitably) heir to the epistemological paradigm of modernity that Kant did but systematize, showing (or thinking to show) that what the Latins had called *ens reale* (being in its finite-mind-independent aspects) was unknowable, while what the Latins had called *ens rationis* (being as dependent upon mental representations through and through, "finite-mind-dependent being") alone constitutes the sphere of human knowledge properly so-called.

Perfectly in line with this epistemological heritage in philosophy (which Sebeok would soon enough brush aside as capable of providing at best no more than the "midmost target" of semiotics),[2] Saussure envisioned the new "science of signs" in exclusively cultural terms, and proposed as its foundation or focal developmental point the linguistic sign—but according to a very special conception thereof. When most people hear of the "arbitrariness" of words, they spontaneously

---

[1] See Deely 2001: Chap. 14, esp. 601–603.
[2] Sebeok 1991: 2.

think of the connection or application of words to things—food, buildings, trees—in our surroundings. Thus, when Saussure says the sign consists of a *signifiant* or "signifier" and a *signifié* or "signified" related "arbitrarily", people are inclined to think of words applied to things.

But "words applied to things" is *not at all* what Saussure intended with his dyadic model of sign consisting of *signifiant/signifié*. Saussure was interested exclusively in the relationship of the word to the mental representations, the ideas or images, in the "minds" of speakers, not individually, but as these form the whole of *langue*, the linguistic system, which he conceived as a kind of autonomous whole unto itself laterally linked infinitely by analogies expressing more in the mind of even the individual speaker than that of which the speaker is fully aware. "Things" in the sense of objects signified (significates), as, for example, when in a restaurant ordering a steak to be prepared medium rare, and then being satisfied or unsatisfied with the steak finally presented (as it were) "in the flesh": that was no part of the *signifié* in Saussure's sense. Objects signified as things had no formal place in the Saussurean semiology/semiotics system.[3]

Keep in mind that, as pointed out above, Saussure's model dominated both Eastern and Western European thinking about signs, but that only in the West, and only partially even there, did his term "semiology" prevail.[4] Apart from Poinsot's outline of the requirements for thematically studying the sign which appeared only in Latin the year of John Locke's birth, but of which the moderns were completely oblivious, the earliest proposal we have within modern philosophy for a science of signs came to publication in the last month of 1689, but bearing the date of 1690, as the concluding chapter of Locke's famous *Essay concerning Humane Understanding*. There he proposed for this "science which does not yet exist but has its place marked out in advance" the name Σημιωτική; and, as we noted above, it was this name that Lotman chose for the first three issues of his journal, *Sign Systems Studies*,[5] the

---

[3] Oddly, from a fully semiotic point of view (i.e., from within the major tradition), the crippling weakness of this omission within a *patron général* supposed as foundational is regarded by some as a core strength of semiology, the foundation of the "Autonomie du langage", as Serra put it in her syllabus for a 2005–06 "Introduction à la Linguistique Générale" (http://www.unil.ch/webdav/site/ling/shared/IntroductionLing/Serra/Intr.a_la_ling.Cours_n_8.pdf): "le signe linguistique a pour fonction de relier un signifiant (image acoustique) à un signifié (concept) et non de relier une expression à un objet du monde".

[4] See Cobley 2009.

[5] Until someone pointed out that Locke's spelling is syntactically deficient from the standpoint of Greek grammar, after which *Sign Systems Studies* adopted the spelling actually incorrect (as it turned out) for Locke's purpose, namely,

oldest semiotics journal on our planet, even though he otherwise embraced Saussure's dyadic model as the stipulative basis for the "new science".

Σημείωτική, as Locke bequeathed the term to name this "new science" had no direct Latin counterpart (though Locke himself did say it was a synonym for "doctrine of signs", the expression used by Poinsot and common among the Latins); but it transliterates into Latin as *Semiotica*, the name of today's foremost international journal of semiotics, as it happens; and *semiotica* from Latin to English, as also Locke's Greek original, yields *semiotics*. Choosing Locke's name but Saussure's model for the new development, Lotman identified *langue* as the "primary modeling system", itself in turn opening the way to and making possible the cultural world or system as a whole, which Lotman termed accordingly the "secondary modeling system". And Lotman's work formed the centerpiece for the development of so-called "Soviet Semiotics", in terminological contrast with, yet foundationally identical to, *semiology* in the West.

Here we need to consider also yet a third thinker seminal to the Saussurean-based development, Algirdas Greimas (9 March 1917–1992 February 27). Like Lotman, Greimas accepted the Saussurean notion of sign, but especially as developed and mediated in the work of Louis Hjelmslev (3 October 1899–1965 May 30), still marking no place of a sign as "natural"; for also like Lotman, Greimas preferred the name "semiotics" to the name "semiology"—though perhaps for quite different reasons.

Anne Hénault, a close assistant to Greimas over many years up to his death, recently suggested to me that the "over the top" usage to which Roland Barthes (12 November 1915–1980 March 25) put the term "semiology" in his 1964 *Éléments de sémiologie* motivated Greimas to put some distance between his own scientific approach to signs and Barthes' metaphorical exaggerations. Be this as it may, Greimas, notwithstanding his semiological foundations and notion of sign, constantly preferred to work under the title of semiotics. Alexandros Lagopoulos, in a letter dated 12 July 2009, pointed out to me that, in the Greimas and Courtés *Dictionary* of 1982, the same entry "Semiology" which waxes "quite dithyrambic about Barthes" also suggests rather clearly that "Greimas opts for the term 'semiotics'" both "because of the relation of the term 'semiology' with a very limited interpretation of Saussure's definition, which sees the system as excluding the semiotic process and thus the signifying practices", and because of the relation of that term "with a narrow application of the linguistic model".

Σημείωτική; but that is another story (Deely 2004) we have not the space to retell here.

Well, the two accounts of Hénault and Lagopoulos are hardly incompatible. And it remains that the question of *what a sign is*, as a distinctive sort of being with a consequently distinctive sort of action, is not merely a question of what *we decide to mean by sign* as a matter of stipulation.[6] Required rather is a cenoscopic and prescissive analysis of our *experience* of the working of signs in order to derive from that action a "guess at the riddle" of what a sign *is* in the distinctiveness of its being contrastive alike with objects and things. Such an investigation, not simply an initial stipulation taken as foundation without further ado, has to be at the center of any inquiry with a claim to being scientific—whether cenoscopically, ideoscopically, or (as is usually the case with semiotics) an interactive combination of the two.

2.2. The Challenge to Saussure's Stipulative Foundation

There had been, in fact, another 20th century thinker, slightly older than Saussure, who agreed with Saussure in principle that a science of signs had a right to existence and its own distinctive thematic place; but he never made Saussure's mistake of thinking that a model of sign activity taken from human culture should be the *"patron général"*. The thinker in question was an American (the only American so far, as I think, who deserves a mention in the front ranks of philosophers), Charles Sanders Peirce (10 September 1839–1914 April 19), whose foundational work in semiotics traces to 1867. The term most frequently used by Peirce was *semiotic*, not "semeiotic" as his epigones have tried to claim.[7]

But Peirce and his work did not figure directly in the widespread semiology/semiotics of early to mid-20th century Saussurean inspiration. Not at all. Interest in Peirce's work was confined mainly to small circles of philosophy students in the United States. Many, perhaps

---

[6] Exactly here do we confront squarely the superiority of the semiotic approach Peirce shares with Poinsot as his main predecessor in uncovering the triadically relational character of semiosis. "What is the essential difference between a sign that is communicated to a mind, and one that is not so communicated? If the question were simply what we do mean by a sign, it might soon be resolved. But that is not the point. We are in the situation of a zoölogist who wants to know what ought to be the meaning of 'fish' in order to make fishes one of the great classes of vertebrates" (Peirce 1904: CP 8.332, italic added; cf. Poinsot 1632: TDS I.1, 116/1–13, 117/20–118/18, etc.). Where the semiologist wants to assert what a sign is, and proceed from there, the semiotician prefers rather first to determine what a sign is, and proceed from there. (It is one of those many and recurrent choices between Nominalism and Scholastic Realism).

[7] See following note.

most, of these students did not tend to see Peirce's work primarily in the perspective of a doctrine of signs (Max Fisch [1900–1995], above all, as the 20th century *doyen* of Peirce scholarship was to change this general inappreciation for semiotics as providing the principal arc of Peirce's intellectual development[8]). They saw Peirce's work rather mainly through the lens of modern philosophy's established categorizations and in terms of the influence on James and Dewey in the "pragmatism" from which, ironically in the case, Peirce eventually came to dissociate himself.[9] Quite specifically, Peirce introduced the term "pragmaticism" to denote the *incompatibility* of his thought with the denial of mind-independent status to relations in which he (rightly)[10] deemed Nominalism of whatever variety—as specifically to include the "pragmatism" of James and Dewey—to consist.[11] One American who did early see Peirce mainly in semiotic terms and developed his thought accordingly was Charles W. Morris (23 May 1903–1979 January 15). The Peircean influence on Morris was transmitted to one of his students, Thomas Albert Sebeok (9 November 1920–2001 December 21), himself a linguist, and a devoted student also of the Russian linguist Roman Osipovich Jakobson (11 October 1896–1982 July 18),[12] who as well prompted Sebeok with an interest in

---

[8] Less commendable was Fisch's responsibility for the myth that Peirce's preferred term for the doctrine of signs was "semeiotic" with no final "s" (pronounced "see-my-OH-tick"), a myth that cannot survive a full survey of Peirce's texts, which shows rather a preference for "semiotic" or "semeiotics": see Deely 2009: 62–65, "3. Clearing the Mists of a Terminological Mythology"; also available online through the Peirce-L archive: <http://www.cspeirce.com/menu/library/aboutcsp/deely/clearing.pdf>.

[9] See "Pragmaticism is not pragmatism", 616–618, and "Pragmaticism and the doctrine of signs", 625–628, in Deely 2001.

[10] See Deely 2001: passim; and 2008.

[11] Peirce died far too early to include the "pragmatism" of Richard Rorty (4 October 1931–2007 June 8). But it remains as one of history's ironies that the nominalist-compatible version of late modern philosophical thought generally known as "pragmatism", a current which prevails from James through Rorty, provides the Peirce-originated but later-replaced name adhered to in presenting even Peirce's distinctive thought among students who should well know better. Cf. Deely 1998a (at <http://www.helsinki.fi/science/commens/papers/redbook.pdf>) and Houser 2006.

[12] Jakobson—"one of the first Soviet scholars who became famous abroad", as Voigt 1995: 201 noted—was certainly deeply schooled in the Tartu-Moscow line of semiotics, of which Lotman was the chief representative. But Jakobson, unlike Lotman, had not remained confined in that world of "nightmarish Soviet bureaucratic restrictions" for most of his career. Indeed, Sebeok had regularly visited with Jakobson at Princeton during his graduate studies, and considered Jakobson his actual if not official Ph.D. thesis director.

Peirce. And it was Peirce, never Saussure, whom Sebeok came eventually to regard as "our lodestar" (as Sebeok put it in his 1984 Presidential Address to the Semiotic Society of America[13]).

The challenge to Saussurean epistemological foundations for developing the new "science of signs", thus, did not come from Peirce directly. It came, as a sociological reality and direct intellectual challenge, from the work of Thomas Sebeok.[14]

If we regard Saussurean semiotics/semiology today as, at worst, a last gasp of modern philosophical idealism and, at best, as a part of the larger "doctrine of signs" that found its most fecund (if not most famous) late 19th-early 20th century exponent in the work of Peirce—and if the name *semiotics* has come quite to displace "semiology" in the countries of Western Europe and North America—it is to Sebeok that we must directly look, and initially to Peirce only indirectly, as well as largely through the Sebeokan influence which has, more than any other, made of semiotics a "global phenomenon" of postmodern intellectual culture, wherein Peirce at last comes directly to influence the discussion. Only now, after Sebeok's successful challenge to the Saussurean semiology/semiotics as a "pars pro toto fallacy",[15] does

---

Lotman's early critique of the Saussurean model in terms of the secondary indexicality necessarily entangled with the "arbitrariness" to which Saussure gave sole emphasis (see Deely 2009c), together with his growing interest in Peirce, were major influences on Sebeok over the many years of his close friendship and intellectual association with Lotman. It is perhaps a striking testimony to just how closed was the "world" of Soviet semiotics, lived from within, that Ivanov (2008) is able to present his "Semiotics of the 20th century" to a Moscow congress without a single mention of Sebeok or of the development of the major tradition outside that insular "Soviet" intellectual universe created on Saussure's "arbitrary model". (Ivanov's survey makes a rather startling contrast with, for example, Sebeok 1998.) It is as if an inadvertent testimony that the originally Saussurean "Moscow-Tartu school" is indeed a thing of the past, especially if we compare it to the emergence after Sebeok of what should be called the "Tartu-Bloomington-Copenhagen school" of biosemiotics today, as will be discussed below, p. 29f. and 95ff.

[13] Sebeok 1984b: 9.

[14] And even Poinsot's work, which first laid the ground systematically for study of signs as triadically relational in being, would not be with us today as an independent study were it not for the initiatives of Thomas A. Sebeok (Sebeok 1986b).

[15] Unfortunately, while Sebeok's campaign to demonstrate the inadequacy of the semiological paradigm (the purely cultural view of sign activity) did have the effect in the West of a virtual abandonment of the term "semiology" as a name for the semiotic enterprise, his program did not have equal success in persuading adherents of the semiological view of sign-action to admit the partial and limited status their analytical approach to the codes of cultural

Peirce in the 20th century's second half begin to emerge within semiotics (beyond the small circle of philosophy students) as a central figure—at first as if alongside, but eventually quite to eclipse, Saussure. The good reason for the eclipsing I will discuss in Section 2.6 following.

But first let it be well understood that, speaking of semiotics as it came best to be understood in the 21st century, the summary statement of W. C. Watt on this point is definitive (2009):[16]

> Sebeok was the re-founder of the discipline, in 1962, and remained its universally-acknowledged *doyen* until his unwelcome death, at 81, at the end of 2001.

2.3. Shifting the Semiotic Enterprise to an Adequate Foundation

Sebeok's challenge to the culture-bound model of semiotics, as common to Saussure, Lotman, Hjelmslev, Greimas, and (originally) Eco, developed in stages; and it was the frustrated biologist in Sebeok himself, not any direct Peircean influence, that was mainly responsible for launching the revolution. However species-specifically unique and over-riding in importance linguistic communication may be among human animals, Sebeok simply deemed it ridiculous to think that the larger matter of the action of signs can be confined to the sphere of culture, or adequately analyzed on the basis of any specific type of sign which is confined to the one species of animal that we designate "human".

To make this point, Sebeok began by proposing the term *zoösemiotics* (he himself did not use the dieresis, although he fully agreed with its semantic point) as a name for the broader study of signs as their action—called semiosis, after Peirce—is found throughout the animal kingdom. There are indeed species-specifically distinctive dimensions of sign action and use among human animals, Sebeok emphasized; but this is also true for animals in every species, and we cannot—as would-be students of the sign wherever its influence is to be traced—blind ourselves to a larger action of signs which overlaps anthroposemiosis but extends beyond human culture in the lifeworlds of other animals.

---

phenomena occupied within the semiotic enterprise as a whole. More than a few Western authors adopted the term "semiotics" as a kind of mask for their work, while continuing to promote a purely semiological enterprise. An outstanding example of this shift from "pars pro toto fallacy" to "pars pro toto masquerade" is Chandler 2002, a book proclaiming to treat of *Semiotics. The Basics* while treating in fact of Semiology. Some "basics", inasmuch as the work considers nothing beyond the cultural side of anthroposemiotics (without even indicating that there is another side: see gloss on this book in the References following).

[16] Watt 2009.

2.4. Remodeling Anthroposemiosis as the Human Use of Signs

Here we come to a truly remarkable syncretism. Sebeok, born Hungarian but American by adoption, saw in the work of two thinkers of the University of Tartu, Estonia—namely, Jakob von Uexküll (8 September 1864–1944 July 25), Estonian/German, and Juri Lotman, Russian/Estonian—the elements in need of synthesis to provide an adequate foundation for the development of semiotics in its contemporary guise, even apart from Peirce (and I will take up the Peircean influence as Sebeok conveyed it shortly). Von Uexküll was what Sebeok termed a "cryptosemiotician". This term provides a crucial category for demarcating the epochs or periods in the development of semiotics (see Deely 2006a). It designates a thinker who, contrary to his or her epistemological paradigm inherited as a modern, nonetheless did work that requires to be re-thought in the perspective of semiotics for the importance of the work fully to be appreciated. In his pioneering study of Umwelt as the meaningful world of objects developed species-specifically by every animal, von Uexküll had been forced to postulate as correlate with the Umwelt the animal Innenwelt, and it was here that Sebeok was able to point out the truly *"primary* modeling system" for anthropsemiosis as a whole.[17]

Sebeok, already in 1970, had gone out of his way to meet in person with Lotman. In 1977 he had made Lotman an Honorary Member of the Semiotic Society of America, under Article 4, Section 1.d. of the SSA Constitution. But it was only after "a protracted dinner" with Lotman on 3 October 1986 in Bergen, Norway (Lotman's "first journey ever to the West")—where what Sebeok describes (1998: 23) as "a mutual rapport and sympathy came to suffuse and envelop us as if we had been the oldest of friends"—that Sebeok came away with the full inspiration for the Uexküll-Lotman (or "Umwelt-Semiosphere") synthesis that was to be a crucial step toward his vision of semiotics as encompassing the whole of life ("biosemiotics").[18]

---

[17] Deely 2001b was the first synthesis of Sebeok's ideas on this point of reinterpreting Jakob von Uexküll's work in explicitly semiotic perspective, and was delivered in an Imatra paper with Sebeok in attendance. After that session Sebeok referred inquirers to the essay as "the best development of von Uexküll's work in explicitly semiotic terms". A further detailed synthesis emphasizing the Innenwelt side of the Umwelt/Innenwelt juxtaposition is set out in Deely 2007, online at <http://www.augustoponzio.com/Critical/12._Deely.pdf>; and in deely 2007.

[18] In conjunction with the private dinner mentioned above, Lotman's public address (1987 publication) to that Norsk Forening for Semiotikk "Symposium on Semiotics in Theory and Practice", organized by Dinda Gorlée and Sven Storelv, had also played a role in inspiring Sebeok's idea for

Returning from that 1986 occasion, Sebeok diplomatically launched his proposal to consider the animal Innenwelt as the primary modeling system for all cognitive life forms, with species-specifically human linguistic communication construed as an exaptation therefrom enabling the further development of culture as the "tertiary modeling system". He began this "diplomatic initiative" in a formal address to the Semiotic Society of America,[19] a basic text that appeared afterward in many places[20] in testimony of the importance for semiotic understanding that Sebeok attached to his new synthesis of the modeling perspective—as would further appear in his later work with Danesi.[21] This Uexküll-Lotman-Sebeok synthesis, it is not too much to say, has become the main foundation-stone for the postmodern development of semiotics. But it is not the whole story of Sebeok's founding (or re-founding) contribution, not by any means.

2.5. Furthering the Foundation: an Action of Signs Beyond the Animal Umwelt

In 1981 Sebeok had already taken the further step of promoting the work of Martin Krampen, whose analysis extended the action of signs beyond even the animal Umwelt to include the realm of plants, not only in relation to animals but among the plants themselves as forms of life. This was a move, patently, that put in place the possibility of proposing biosemiotics. It is rather astonishing to realize that Augustine, in his original proposal for a general notion of sign as transcending the ancient nature/culture divide, expressly pointed to this same possibility of semiosis among plants as a "motus animi" communicated to neighboring plants![22]

---

this remarkable Innenwelt/Umwelt + Semiosphere synthesis, toward which he hoped to directly enlist Lotman himself, as he tells us (Sebeok 1998: 31): "Lotman, in his introductory speech, righly underlined the contemporary emergence of syncretic tendencies ... in semiotic investigations. 'In the humanities', he said, 'different disciplines combine into a single science of man, centered around the semiotic study of culture.' Commute science for the humanities, life for man, and nature for culture—and this great, charismatic thinker and I might have consummated a transcendental disputation. I had hoped to argue my case, and ancillary issues, at our next scheduled encounter, at the 25th Symposium of the Tartu-Moscow School of Semiotics, held in Imatra, Finland, 27–29 July 1987 (Sebeok 1988), but, alas, Lotman could not attend, and I never saw him again."

[19] See Sebeok 1987, his first presentation to the Semiotic Society of America subsequent to the Lotman meeting.

[20] See Sebeok 1988, 1988a, 1989a, 1991a, 1991b.

[21] Sebeok and Danesi 2000.

[22] On this amazing point, see Deely 2006 and 2009b.

Worth noting is the fact that two pioneers of the biosemiotics development have also been named "Thomas A. Sebeok Fellows" of the Semiotic Society of America, one of the most distinguished awards in semiotics today. The Danish semiotician, Jesper Hoffmeyer (21 February 1942–), was named in 2000 the Fourth Sebeok Fellow, precisely because of his 1996 pioneering book on the expansion of semiotic understanding to include the action of signs throughout the sphere of life (see now his 2008a claim that biology itself is but "immature biosemiotics"). Then, also for pioneering work in biosemiotics, the Estonian semiotician, Kalevi Kull (12 August 1952–), was in 2003 named the Fifth Sebeok Fellow.

When we consider Sebeok's pioneering role—both in synthesizing the theoretical work developed at Tartu University by the German Estonian Jakob von Uexküll at the beginning of the 20th century with the work done there by the Russian Estonian Juri Lotman at the end of the 20th century, and in laying the foundations of biosemiotics generally, together with his promotion of the biosemiotic work of Kull and Hoffmeyer both in issues of the journal *Semiotica* and in his book series—it is hard to avoid speaking today rather of a "Tartu-Bloomington-Copenhagen school" as having succeeded the earlier "Tartu-Moscow school";[23] and it is the former "school" which has provided the main theoretical thrust within the biosemiotics development up through the first decade of the 21st century.[24]

But let us not get too far ahead of ourselves. What needs to be noted here is that, around this same time that Sebeok promoted the idea of a "phytosemiotics" (with his publication of Krampen 1981), he also became particularly vocal in declaring to all with ears to hear that the so-far mainstream contemporary semiology/semiotics of the 20th century's first half or so was guilty of incarnating a "Pars pro Toto" fallacy—the very fallacy recently turned on its head and reintroduced within biosemiotics, as we shall shortly comment in pp. 35-36 below. *Frontiers in Semiotics*[25] was the volume that landed Sebeok's "pars pro toto" point squarely in the mainstream North American semiotic literature of the period.

2.6. The Place of Peirce, after Poinsot, in Displacing the *Pars Pro Toto* Fallacy

Peirce's view of semiotics in the end proved even broader than Sebeok's.[26] If we ask ourselves why Sebeok nonetheless came to regard

---

[23] See esp. Appendix, pp. 95-97 below.

[24] See further in Section 2.10. pp. 42-45; then most fully in subsection 3.6.5.,p. 63f., and Appendix, p. 95ff.

[25] Deely, Williams, and Kruse, eds. 1986.

[26] See Deely 1989: "Peirce's Grand Vision" concerning an action of signs

Peirce as "our lodestar" for the development of semiotics,[27] we do not have far to seek for the answer. Semiosis, Peirce said, is the name for the action of signs that follows upon their distinctive being; so "semiotics", Sebeok said along with Peirce, is the name for the knowledge that results from the identification and study of that distinctive way of acting (semiosis), wherever it is to be found. Just as biology is the name for the study of the action of living beings, so semiotics is the name for the study of the action of signs. But here is where Peirce set himself apart from Saussure and all the followers of Saussure, and apart also from all those who would think that we need but transfer a code-based model from culture to biology in order to have an adequate foundation for biosemiotics, the study of semiosis as presupposed for all living things, not just animals.

"*If the question*" *of semiotics* "*were simply what we do mean by a sign*", *Peirce presciently remarked,*[28] "*it might soon be resolved.*" *But stipulation or decree is not the means by which any science, cenoscopic or ideoscopic, achieves its fundamental goals.* Not at all. As semioticians, Peirce noted, we are rather "in the situation of a zoölogist who wants to know what ought to be the meaning of 'fish' in order to make fishes one of the great classes of vertebrates"—how is it that "a sign is something by knowing which we know something more"? That is the question. Our point of departure is not simply the common understanding of what some particular thing is as "a sign", but the question of what is sign such that it is able to function in the manner that we experience it as functioning—revealing nature, stitching together culture and nature, real and unreal relations, weaving the fabric of experience, and leading us down blind alleys and cul-de-sacs as well as broad avenues of being and nonbeing in the forests of human belief:[29]

> We all have a ragged-outlined notion of what we call a sign. We wish to replace that by a well-defined concept, which may exclude some things ordinarily called signs, and will almost certainly include some things not ordinarily so-called.

There we have the distinctiveness of Peirce in the matter of semi-

---

throughout the universe. Sebeok, as far as I know, first proposed his co-extensivity of sign-science and life-science in his address entitled "The Sign Science and the Life Science" to the Hungarian Academy of Sciences on 1 October 1990, which I had the privilege to attend. In 1991, at Tom's invitation, I published my argument against this thesis; at the time of his death a decade after, we were still in discussion of the issues.

[27] Sebeok 1984b: 9.

[28] Peirce 1904: CP 8.332, italic added.

[29] Peirce 1905: EP 2.388.

otics, as also of Poinsot well before him: the recognition that signs lead us everywhere in nature as well as in culture, including, as Claus Emmeche puts it,[30] where humans "have never set foot".

Instead of taking some particular kind of sign as paradigm, and basing everything on that particular notion, as Saussure proposed, Peirce took instead exactly the path that Poinsot had blazed in 1632 to open *his* inquiry into sign: **What is it that makes a sign, regardless of the particular type of its vehicle in nature or in culture, actually to be a sign?** And both men arrived at the identical answer: the sensible phenomena that we *call* "signs" are such only by reason of occupying the foreground position of representing another than themselves to or for some third. **A sign—any sign—is a sign by virtue of a relation irreducibly triadic attaining that which it signifies directly and an interpretant indirectly as its "proper significate outcome".**

Now relations have never been well understood in modern thought, ever since Ockham postulated that only individuals exist, and that "relations" arise only when there are two or more individuals similar in some feature(s) according to a comparison made by some observer, in some mind. Apart from mind there are only the individuals interacting. So if signs really consist in relations, then Ockham's model fits well the notion that only in human culture are there signs. But if relations are indifferently mind-independent, *ens reale*, or mind-dependent, *ens rationis*, depending only upon the surrounding circumstances, as Poinsot called to our attention, then we can see at once how signs transcend, as suprasubjective relations, all the divisions of subjective and physical being, not only the nature/culture divide, but also the inner/outer, self/other, psychological/physical divides as well.

A causal relation, for example, in modern thought, is considered as the interaction of two or more things. But such interaction is not a relation; a relation is what results from and survives as over and above the interaction. A relation is invisible to sense, even though it unites the sensed; and it is indifferent to spatial distance, unlike the interaction which gave rise to it.

All of this, then, enters into our semiotic notion of sign. A sign as provenating a triadic relation is not an object, or at least need not be. On the contrary, the action of signs—semiosis—is what every object presupposes.[31] And just as any given thing may or may not be an object, but as object directly is normally *not* a Saussurean *signifié* (and *never* by way of a relation other than triadic in any event), so we may

---

[30] Emmeche 1994: 126.

[31] The argument for this "semiotic sign" notion (Deely 2004a) has now been presented in dramatic reading form on YouTube: <http://www.youtube.com/view_play_list?p=E9651802BCDC14BF>.

say that what Poinsot and Peirce call an "object signified" (which turns out simply to be a redundant and clumsy way to say significate) actually has no place directly within a semiological scheme.

And here we reach the heart of the matter: code-based sign-analyses, no matter how many "things" they may involve, three or a hundred and three, are reducibly dyadic combinations, whereas the being that makes a sign a sign remains irreducibly triadic as well as suprasubjective—even when the significate is purely objective[32] and not a thing at all.

And this indirectness involved in the being of signs as triadic relations is precisely what explains the main—the overwhelming—difference between semiosic causality and all other forms of causality: while other forms of causality can take place only between actually existing and present things, semiosic causality can take place even when one (or sometimes two) of the elements united under the triadic relation don't exist now, or perhaps never did or never will exist. No other causality can compete with that; and that singularity of signs as relations (i.e., of signs considered in their proper and distinctive being as signs) is precisely why semiosis in nature acts as a *vis a prospecto*—a real but indirect possibility of the future influencing the relation of past things to the here and now arrangements of things in the present— even alongside the *vis a tergo* so beloved of reductionist biologists such as Dennett and Dawkins (among many).

So the action of signs depends upon, because indeed it follows upon, the *being* of signs; and that being in every instance involves something of subjectivity (normally in its vehicle), but transcends that subjectivity as well in uniting it with other subjectivities and objectivities in the process and web of semiosis, a web precisely of *relations* at once suprasubjective and triadically unifying the vehicle of the signification directly with its significate and indirectly with an interpretant "which need not be mental".

Code-based analyses, in Peirce's terms, reduce to Secondness. Signs do not, because signs *are* not only relations but also relations triadic in type. Whence "Thirdness is the triadic relation", Peirce tells us[33]—in this merely echoing Poinsot[34]—"considered as constituting the mode of being of a sign." Hence code-based semiotics, be they applied in the realm of culture or in the realm of biological nature, are a *pars*, never the *totum*, of semiotic analysis; and when mistaken for the whole of the semiotic story such analyses constitute a fallacy—no less in the 21st century's biosemiotic development than in the mid-20th century's

---

[32] Deely 2009c.
[33] Peirce 1904: CP 8.332.
[34] Poinsot 1632: 154/25–29.

exclusively cultural semiology / semiotics. Coding and code-based outcomes unquestionably have a place in the semioses of living things
(there is a place in biosemiotics for biosemiology as a part, just as there
is a place in anthroposemiotics for semiology as a part); but that place
is not the whole, still less is it the main part of the story of semiotics as
the doctrine (the cenoscopic science) of signs.

2.7. Setting the Record Straight on What Semiotics Is All About

Semiotics is the knowledge developed by studying the action of signs
and all that that action involves, including codes. But the action of
signs as such springs from the being of signs as triadic relations, and
that is not a question at all of "Peirce versus Saussure". Biosemiotics is
no more "Peircean" than biology is "Darwinian". Personalities shape
and influence but do not constitute scientific domains in their objectivity. Biosemiotics is the study of the action of signs in the living world,
just as biology is the study of organisms. Indeed, insofar as biology to
this point has tended to recognize only *vis a tergo*, while semiotics has
been able to identify in addition *vis a prospecto* at work in the interactions of living things (Hoffmeyer's "semiotic scaffolding", for
example), it may even be the case, as recently argued by Hoffmeyer,[35]
that "biology is immature biosemiotics". It is ironic that the *pars pro toto*
fallacy of 20th century cultural semiotics should now by some be reintroduced into the 21st century semiotics of the biological world. This
amounts to semiology "turned on its head", somewhat as Marx is said
to have done with Hegel's dialectic.

As semiology can be regarded *either* as a part of the larger whole of
semiotics *or* as a last gasp of the modern idealist doctrine that the mind
itself makes whatever the mind comes to know, so code-based biosemiotics proposed as a larger whole than sign-based biosemiotics
misunderstands the very foundation of the whole semiotic enterprise,
and repeats the *pars pro toto* fallacy of semiology all over again. Code-
based biosemiotics can assume a rightful place within and as an
essential part of semiosis-based biosemiotics, or it can delude itself as
being a larger whole. In either case, it is *biosemiology* that we are con-
fronted with when codes become our paradigm, not biosemiotics in the
proper sense of the body of knowledge being developed from study of
the action of signs within the whole of the living world.

2.8. "Science" or "Doctrine" of Signs?

In that 18th century burgeoning of European thought we call the
Enlightenment, thinkers were mainly animated by the idea that the new

---

[35] Hoffmeyer 2008a, title.

science, based on experimentation and mathematization of results (science in the modern sense, ideoscopically developed inquiries), would "slow by slow" displace and replace all previous human knowledge.

It took some centuries for thinkers to begin to start to commence to realize that this was by no means possible, for the excellent reason that if the whole of the knowledge we acquire before becoming scientists has no independent validity, then science itself would have no validity. Yet even today, *by no means* have all thinkers awakened from the Enlightenment "dream of reason",[36] as we witness in those who would set philosophy off to one side as otiose for the future of semiotics. (Recall that Berkeley pointed out to the early moderns that primary qualities could not be known as belonging to things if the secondary qualities upon which the knowledge depended were purely mind-dependent representations; but sometimes points obvious to the point of self-evident—such as the verification theory's claim that verification constituted meaning, to pick a recent circularity—take human animals centuries to realize. Some still think, to pick another recent example, that Frege's sense/reference distinction resolves the problem of objectivity!)

Unfortunately, in the past, we had no better name than common sense for the "prior knowledge" from which science in the modern sense begins and which it presupposes throughout its investigations; and if ever a notion has been discredited beyond possibility of rehabilitation it is surely the notion of common sense. We owe again a great deal to Peirce in this regard, drawing on Bentham (of all people!) for showing that "common sense" is not necessarily common, but that neither is science necessarily ideoscopic, but cenoscopic as well—and presuppositively.

For semiotics, the most basic of the cenoscopic sciences, has now succeeded in showing that the whole of human knowledge, from its animal beginnings in sense[37] through its development in imagination,

---

[36] Notable in this regard is Gottlieb 2001, whose book is not for nothing described as "a stunning successor" to Bertrand Russell's 1945 *History*.

[37] Sensation is to animals, we may say (I owe the analogy to Kalevi Kull), what root systems are to plants. When Barbieri says (2009: 164) that "single cells do not build internal representations of the world and therefore cannot interpret them", he quite amply displays his lack of understanding of the distinction between interpretant and interpreter. Again when he says that "animals react only to representations of the world", he manifests his tacit beholdenness to Kantian epistemology in exactly the sense that semiotics begins by surpassing. As early as Poinsot's dazzling analysis in 1632 of why animal sensation prescissively considered within perception ("phantasiari", actually, for which we have no full equivalent in the modern languages, though "perception" comes the closest) is already a web of semiosic relations, even though no mental representation is yet involved, the doctrine of signs had made clear that not only is representation not the whole story of mental life, much less

memory, and estimation, and its further extensions in intellection as not reducing to objects perceptually instantiable as such, depends upon the action of signs. So what are we to call this knowledge, which is derived analytically without being dependent upon the experimentation that typifies science in the modern sense? It is, Peirce tells us,[38] a science, yes, but one that is *cenoscopic* first of all, and only secondarily an *ideoscopic* science.[39]

Now this—cenoscopy and ideoscopy as subtended by cenoscopy—is a terminology that has only recently begun to be taken up and developed. If we look back over the centuries, however, we find that the word *scientia* in the Latin age, when (practically speaking) only cenoscopic science existed (and at that in a state which confused all too readily "common sense" conclusions concerning points which required, if not ideoscopy, as least prescissive care in handling), has a Latin synonym, namely, *doctrina*. It is interesting that this synonym for science as cenoscopic is precisely the one that Sebeok, as early as 1976,[40] expressed a strong preference for over the Saussurean-inspired label "science of signs", where the word "science" clearly carried its modern ideoscopic sense.

It was not that there were no key figures contemporary with Sebeok, such as Paul Bouissac, seeking to push semiotics wholly in the direction of ideoscopy.[41] Indeed, no one more than Sebeok appreciated the importance of ideoscopic results, including for the development of

---

of semiotics, but that other-representation is prior alike to the self-representation of things in sense-perception and to the self-representation of objects in experience more generally, including the cases of illusion or mistaken identity where the object self-represented is not what it seems.

[38] Pierce 1908: CP 8.343.

[39] Peirce borrowed this cenoscopic/idioscopic distinction from Bentham (see Deely 2001a: 618n21). Ashley (2006: 85–87), giving a fine illustration of the applicability of this distinction as Peirce drew it, uses the variant spelling "ideoscopic", which is therefore not to be confused with Peirce's usage of the term "ideoscopic", which concerns the phaneron rather than (as in Ashley) idioscopy proper. I am indebted to Ransdell (1997: note 1). Ashley's spelling of "ideoscopic, ideoscopy" as synonymous with Peirce's spelling as "idioscopic, idioscopy" is discussed in Deely 2003 and especially in 2008.

[40] In his "Preface" to *Contributions to the Doctrine of Signs*; see in particular the entry that he later commissioned for the *Encyclopedic Dictionary of Semiotics*, ed. Sebeok, Bouissac, Eco, Pelc, Posner, Rey, and Shukman (1st ed.; Berlin: Mouton, 1986), Vol. 1 of 3, p. 214 (=Deely 1986a).

[41] Precisely for this reason, as we remarked in note 17 of Chap. 1, Sebeok arranged to have published side-by-side, as it were, the two competing "manifestos" (as he referred to them privately) on this point concurrently developed in 1984: on the one side by Anderson, Deely, Krampen, Ransdell, Sebeok, and T. von Uexküll, and on the other side by Gardin, Bouissac, and Foote.

semiotics. But Sebeok, unlike Bouissac and other Enlightenment epigones after him, recognized quite well the blunder of continuing to embrace the Enlightenment understanding of the enterprise of modern science being the complete displacement of all cenoscopic with ideoscopic knowledge; and he opted accordingly for the sounder alternative of providing for semiotics a cenoscopic base. This story, indeed (without the later terminology of cenoscopy and ideoscopy) is spelled out in Williams 1985 "review of the reviews" as part of her Preface to the corrected reprinting of Sebeok's key book of 1976.

So the question, "science of signs or doctrine of signs?", admits of no simple-minded solution. For all of science is critically controlled development of human knowledge, whether the framework of that development be primarily ideoscopic and experimental or primarily cenoscopic and directly experiential—or, as in biosemiotics, a fertile admixture of the two. But when we reflect that our intellectual ancestors of Latin times had not one but two terms for "science", and that only one of these—*doctrina*—has retained its predominantly cenoscopic overtones, the fact that this alternate expression, "doctrine of signs", is the one consistently used by preference by every major figure so far in the compelling and still-unfolding semiotic story, from Augustine through Aquinas and Poinsot, to Locke, Peirce, and Sebeok in our own day, takes on considerable historical weight. In opting for Poinsot's, Locke's, and Peirce's "doctrine of signs" over Saussure's "science of signs", what Sebeok was signaling was nothing less or other than Peirce's point that semiotics is first of all a cenoscopic science, and as such provides the framework for the whole of ideoscopy—not only within biosemiotics, but for the whole of academic and intellectual culture.

2.9. Does the Action of Signs Reach Even Beyond the Land of the Living?

Whether there can be any action of signs outside the sphere of living things depends not upon living things but upon the being proper to signs, which is at bottom what determines how signs as such act.[42] What signs are remains the central question that we have seen— throughout our brief review of the 20th century origins of semiotic development through to the 21st century present—code-based analysts beginning with Saussure have avoided to face. Hence they have tended to miss the irreducibility of triadic *relations* which are not "triangles" and cannot be reduced to triangles (or "trinities"), even though the relations in question depend upon and involve the biological agents of interaction in the physical surroundings.

---

[42] See Deely 1990: Chap. 3. More extended treatment in 2009i; also in Chap. 12 of 2009d: 233–275.

Whether the *vis a prospecto* of semiosis as an indirect, probabilistic causality was at work in the world of nature as the universe, beginning as lifeless and incapable of supporting life, moved through a series of transformations which made life more and more possible, indeed likely, and eventually actual, is a question that reductionist interaction models of science do not know how to face. Yet it is precisely the handling of this question, by prescissive analysis, not by declaration or vote, that can alone determine how far the action of signs extends.

Peirce, our lodestar, made his most dramatic move not at all in discovering analytically that without triadic relations there are no signs whatsoever; indeed, this had already been fully demonstrated in Poinsot's work centuries before. No. Peirce's most dramatic move in semiotics was in separating the third term of the sign relation from the order of finite mind, with his distinction between *interpretant* and *interpreter*, and the declaration that an interpretant *need not be mental*. This was the move that sets Peirce apart in the history of philosophy and semiotics as cenoscopic science; and this was the move that led to his famous proposal that "the universe is perfused with signs, if it does not consist exclusively of them".

The view that the universe consists exclusively of signs is the only view that could properly be labeled *pansemiotics* or *pansemiotism*. But if there is a semiosis beyond life, that specific extension calls for a specific term, not a comprehensive one with an historical implication that "all is semiosis". The best term proposed so far for a semiosis at work prior to and independent of life but inevitably preparatory to life and supportive of life once it has emerged is *physiosemiosis*.

There is no limit to the damage that can result from an ill-considered appropriation of such a term as "pansemiotics", the historicity of which is loaded with inevitable meanings from the past conveyed analogically quite beyond the ability of an individual user effectively to control the usage by arbitrary stipulation. Arbitrariness does not trump historicity; it merely feeds upon it.[43] Indeed, there is evidence that this appropriation (or misappropriation) of "pansemiotics" as a term of discussion may already be "going viral". Marc Champagne informs me:[44]

> Todd Oakley writes (in *Cognitive Semiotics* 1, pp. 26–27, 27n2) that "Semiotics is the study of signs produced intentionally by human beings and taken by other human beings as expressions of their producers' conscious mental states and communicative intentions",[45] and

---

[43] See Chapter 6 of *Purely Objective Reality*, "The Sign—Arbitrariness or Historicity" (Deely 2009c: 84–109).

[44] Email of 3 July 2009.

[45] Another colleague, in an email of 9 July 2009 11:38 hours, called this "the single most misguided definition of 'semiotics' ever put to paper", deserving to

states that those who "descend from the anthropological rung" (he cites Sebeok and Hoffmeyer) are—hold on to your armchair— "pansemiotists"!"

However lacking in semiotic sophistication Oakley's assertion may be, it yet serves as a reminder and illustration that terminology is more than arbitrary, and that the "pars pro toto fallacy" is capable of many transformations as it continues to plague discourse about signs.

But that the universe is *perfused* with signs no semiotician today has much—if any—room to doubt. The only question outstanding is in what exactly does this perfusion consist? Is it simply that all things are in principle knowable, but actually to know any of them we depend upon the action of signs? Is it simply that all living things in order to thrive and develop over time depend upon the action of signs? Or is it indeed that the very universe itself, in order to make life possible in the first place, was already partially dependent upon a virtual action of signs where objectivity, too, was only virtual, while things alone were actual and interactive? (This last was an idea already implicit in the Augustinian notion of *signa naturalia*, or physionomic signs, in contrast to the *signa data*, or teleonomic signs, manifestative of life.[46])

It is a fascinating question, one that the indirect formal causality of relations in their suprasubjective being as triadic inevitably poses. Particularly in view of the singularity of semiosic causality, whereby it transpires not only among things that are, but between things that are and things that are not—yet or never, depends; but not only upon the action of signs—it is not surprising that Sebeok, despite his own view that life is the boundary line for the actual beginning of semiosis proper, characterized the first book formally to propose an action of signs in nature prior to as well as accompanying life[47] as "the only successful modern English introduction to semiotics". How far the action of signs extends depends upon the causality proper to signs; and what that causality is depends upon the being proper to signs as signs—my

---

be "cited by semioticians of every stripe as an example of exactly the kind of ignorance that we are up against".

[46] See Deely 2009: 6.4.2. "To Capture Augustine's Initiative in a Terminological Proposal", 55–56, esp. the summary "Table".

[47] Deely 1990, *Basics of Semiotics*, Chapter 6, "Physiosemiosis and Phytosemiosis". The fifth edition of this work (2009d) contains in Chapter 12 (Section 4.1.) a discussion of "Why Sebeok's final view of semiosis as co-extensive with life is not broad enough". On Peirce in this matter, my main comment so far is 1989; on the prospect of physiosemiosis itself, see further 1993a, 1995, 1997, 1998, 1999, 2001a, 2007a, and the first official SSA Session on the topic, "Adventures in Physiosemiosis" with papers by Coletta (197–202) and Newsome (203–207) in Deely and Sbrocchi eds. 2008.

goodness! the very question from which the whole of semiotics (the *totum*, as it were, not just this or that *pars*) arises in the first place!

2.10. Semiotics in the 21st Century's Dawn: Sebeok's Shaping Role

Before transitioning now to as large a picture as we can draw of the contours of semiotics as the emerging future wherein the proponents of semiotics struggle to find the best way or ways to institutionalize the doctrine of signs within the framework of university life as it has been shaped especially over the last three centuries by the institutionalization rather of *specializations* within the academic community, let us summarize the present section with an explicit delineation of the central shaping role of Thomas A. Sebeok in giving to the global development of semiotics today its overall shape or "direction".

Since Saussure's early 20th century kindling of the flame, the study of signs as a "new science" has come a long way, and much has been learned about the question, particularly with respect to what turns out to have been something of an overstatement on Saussure's part, namely, that as of his time the science in question "does not exist". We know now not only that Charles Peirce contemporaneously with Saussure was independently engaged in the same question of establishing a "science of signs", but that he was going about the quest in a much better-informed and broad-based manner—following, in fact, the "properly scientific" procedure recommended by Aristotle throughout his works:[48]

> It is necessary, while formulating the problems of which in our further advance we are to find the solutions, to call into council the views of those of our predecessors who have declared any opinion on this subject, in order that we may profit by whatever is sound in their suggestions and avoid their errors.

Peirce was raised on Kant, and so had in philosophy a quintessentially "modern", i.e., an "epistemological", formation. But he found in the moderns next to nothing of value for penetrating the question of what signs are and how they function or act. So he began to dig further in philosophy's history, becoming thereby, in effect, the first of the moderns to eschew Descartes' advice that the Latins be ignored.

This move had the transforming effect to make of Peirce the "last of the moderns and first of the postmoderns", as I have elsewhere

---

[48] The particular passage I cite is from the *De Anima*, Book I, the opening of Chapter 2, 403b20–23 in the Bekker pagination; but the content of this particular passage is found repeatedly throughout the whole of Aristotle's works.

explained at length;[49] for what Peirce discovered was precisely that our Latin forebears had over many centuries advanced in an understanding of the notion of sign as a distinctive subject matter requiring a scientific treatment of its own. In particular, he found also that the discussion of sign to be fruitful presupposed as its "root notion", so to say, relation as a suprasubjective reality, an idea originally broached by Plato,[50] but fully thematized only in Aristotle's work[51] as later taken up among the Latins and applied specifically to the question of sign. Peirce familiarized himself with the works of Aquinas, Scotus, Ockham, and the Conimbricenses. He developed a particular fondness for Scotus, as the first really to have advanced the realization that psychological states—"concepts" or "ideas"—function cognitively as sign-vehicles. From the Conimbricenses he adopted his famous thesis that "all thought is in signs", and from the Conimbricenses no doubt, Poinsot's teachers,[52] he was put on the trail of the decisive discovery, first fully formulated and set out in demonstrative form by Poinsot in 1632,[53] that a triadic relation is required for any sign-vehicle fully to signify, and hence constitutes the formal and proper being of signs.

Virtually unknown in the matter of signs in the 20th century's first half, when Saussure's stipulated dyadic model for sign came into near-universal adoption as the basis for semiotic discourse, by the 1960s Peircean ideas had begun to emerge from the background and sidelines of semiotic discussion to occupy instead center-stage, with the Saussurean stipulated dyadic model being increasingly displaced by a Peircean triadic relational model uncovered by a prescissive cenoscopic analysis rather than by stipulation or "decree".

But exactly how did this move of Peirce from the sidelines to center-stage come about? The answer to that question lies in the work of one man above all others, the linguist and "biologist manqué" Thomas A. Sebeok. Not only was Sebeok instrumental in bringing Peirce to the foreground of semiotic discourse, but he was also responsible for the major shifts in terminology that accompanied and surrounded this "Peircean emergence".

---

[49] Principally in Deely 2001: esp. Chap. 15; but also earlier, in Deely 2000a: The Green Book <http://www.helsinki.fi/science/commens/papers/greenbook.pdf> and elsewhere.

[50] Esp. in Plato's c.399/390BC middle dialogues "Parmenides", "Phaedo", "Theatetus", but also in the c.359–347BC late dialogue, "Sophist". Cf. Cavarnos 1975: 18–19, and passim.

[51] For a full discussion of Aristotle on this point, see Deely 1985: 472–474, esp. fns. 112–114 for the Greek texts. See also Deely 2001: 73–78, esp. "The category of relation", 73–74.

[52] See Beuchot and Deely 1995: "Common Sources for the Semiotic of Charles Peirce and John Poinsot".

[53] Poinsot 1632: *Tractatus de Signis*, Book I, Question 3.

As Peirce found and Sebeok fully realized (not only through Peirce but also by his support for bringing to publication the semiotic of John Poinsot), "doctrina signorum" is the oldest expression for a general theory of signs. Not only does *doctrina signorum* go back to Augustine and, through him, passes down to Aquinas and finally Poinsot in the first florescence of semiotic consciousness (understood as the achievement of an explicit awareness that the being of signs consists, strictly speaking, in a relation that is not only suprasubjective but also triadic in character), but its English version as "doctrine of signs" was, as we saw, expressly pointed out by John Locke as a synonym for his own neologism to name the subject, "semiotics". In addition, "doctrine of signs" was the expression similarly used by Charles Sanders Peirce in his own investigations of the matter. The upshot of all this is that *doctrine of signs* became the express choice made by Thomas A. Sebeok in his unmasking of Saussure's proposed basic model or *patron général* for the study of signs as a **"pars pro toto fallacy"**.

Thus, Sebeok's twofold establishment in the West—first, that semiotics is not equivalent to semiology as a science based upon Saussure's model of sign as a dyadic and wholly anthropological (or anthropocentrically anthroposemiotic) construction; and, second, that Saussure's proposal of this equivalence was an instance of the "pars pro toto" fallacy—remained largely hidden from Eastern eyes, by virtue of a simple linguistic habit resulting from the adoption in the East of Saussure's *patron général* as linked from the first with the in-principle-broader term "semiotics".[54]

Sebeok far from rested content with his, so to say, "conquest of the West" for semiotics as a *doctrina* (a "cenoscopic science") including culture but only as itself a species-specific part of nature as a larger and comprehensive whole. He was determined to extend his conquest to the East as well, and thus to establish semiotics precisely as *global*[55] within what has proven to be the "postmodern era" of intellectual culture as now dawning. To this end, Sebeok approached Juri Lotman

---

[54] Thus, in 1964, the very year following Sebeok's introduction of the notion of zoösemiotics expanding the understanding of signs beyond the artificial boundary of culture as set for the study by Saussure and his epigones, Juri Lotman established the first semiotics journal, using therefor the very name and spelling originally proposed by Locke: Σημίωτική. Ironically, this correct stipulation for the doctrine of signs after only three issues was "corrected" by later editors to read Σημείωτική—concerning which change it can only be said that "they knew not what they did", as detailed etymological study of the terms in question (Deely 2003a, 2004) amply reveals. But that is a side matter.

[55] See my Preface, "A Global Enterprise", to the 1989 corrected reprinting of Sebeok's 1979 book, *The Sign & Its Masters.* See also Sebeok 2001 and Petrilli 2010.

directly, both reporting on his initial discussions to an annual meeting of the Semiotic Society of America,[56] and expressing full confidence that Lotman would soon enough join him[57] in establishment of the "Tartu-Bloomington synthesis"[58]—as we might call the merger that Sebeok effected of Jakob von Uexküll's Umwelttheorie with Lotman's notion of modeling system—to form the basis for the whole development today of biosemiotics, the study of an action of signs throughout the whole of the living world.

As fate would have it, the joint statement of Sebeok and Lotman, however established in spirit between the two, was never to reach the stage of formal "joint statement", by reason simply, as we may opine, of Lotman's death in 1993. Yet it remains that the shift of semiotic studies from an arbitrary and stipulated model of sign to an experiential and cenoscopic understanding that the sign as vehicle produces its effects by way of an arrangement determined by the position occupied by any given idea, affect, object, or thing within a triadic relation (best explicated theoretically first by John Poinsot in the early 17th century and then again more fully in the evolutionary context of our understanding of the universe today by Charles Sanders Peirce), was established globally through the work and influence of Thomas A. Sebeok.

Susan Petrilli, in the remarks cited in our opening paragraphs that semiotics is "a phenomenon more 'of our time' than it is of any time past", is thus also correct in her view that Thomas A. Sebeok had come to stand as the 20th century "founding father" above all others, the "Master of the masters of sign", by the time the 21st century dawned. We stand squarely in the first quarter of the first fully postmodern century, we may say, insofar as semiotics itself appears more and more distinctly as the positive essence of postmodernity as a philosophical—or, as Peirce would have us say, a cenoscopic—development, the first formation of a community of inquirers into the phenomenon of semiosis.

If today the question of physiosemiosis stands open before us as a "final frontier" in the question of how far does the action of signs extend, it is to Sebeok that owe the general recognition of this frontier, even as we owe to Peirce, thanks to his laying down of the distinction between an *interpreter* and an *interpretant* "which need not be mental"—the initial drawing of this "line in the sand".[59]

---

[56] Sebeok 1987. Recall the discussion on pp.30-31 above.

[57] Sebeok 1998.

[58] As we will in this essay later see (Appendix, p. 95ff.), the full realization of Sebeok's aim in this matter would finally be achieved rather by the achievement of a "Tartu-Bloomington-Copenhagen school", and only some years after his death.

[59] See "Peirce's Grand Vision" (Deely 1989).

2.11. After Sebeok and Beyond:
Completing the Compass of Semiotic Understanding

Reporting on the 9–18 December 2009 "United Nations Climate Change Conference" in Copenhagen, Denmark, Zhao Cheng, Tian Fan, and Wei Dongze comment[60] that "History has shown once again that the biggest challenge of mankind [in the full sense of "humankind"?] is mankind itself." Where exactly in history this point has been proven or repeatedly proven the authors do not say. Yet we can say that nowhere in history has this point been demonstrated with the clarity and thoroughness that semiotics is able to achieve, simply by reason of the fact that the human animal emerges within history as the only animal able to become aware of and directly affect the one process on which the whole of the living world most completely depends, to wit, the action of signs or semiosis, in particular as that action leads to a *knowledge* upon which *control* of things as they are depends over and above (or "beyond") our animal cathexis of them as to our liking (+), dislike (–), or indifference (0). Not all things are signs, any more than all objects are things. But all things, even as all objects, are *knowable* only through and on the basis of an action of signs, which is what makes the consequences of human action upon the environment both something that can be known and something that (through understanding in its technological expressions) can therefore be controlled, which is the source of the "global" human responsibility for human action.

Now traditionally the human responsibility for human action has been termed "ethics", and has been conceived principally if not exclusively with respect to the actions of human beings within the realm of culture. The realization of our larger responsibility for the *whole* of life on earth—sometimes termed "Gaia", not in the ancient mythological sense but in the postmodern sense originally specified by Lovelock (1979 and after)—was slow in dawning. When Aristotle distinguished "speculative understanding" of the nature of things from "practical understanding" of the matters that fall under human control, the heavens were deemed eternal and unchangeable, as were also species on earth. Only individuals, and only earthly individuals, underwent birth and death (more exactly: "generation and corruption"), and the sphere of human control reached its maximum extent in the political control of the affairs of state. This view prevailed to the time of Galileo and Poinsot, when it quickly began to dissolve, a dissolution culminating, we might say, in the aftermath of Darwin's famous work of 1859.

---

[60] Zhao Cheng, Tian Fan, and Wei Dongze 2009: <http://www.fmprc.gov.cn/eng/zxxx/t648096.htm>.

But once it had been discovered that not only earth but the whole of the universe is subject to generation and corruption, that not only individuals but also the very species into which individuals are born "come and go" and develop over time, it could only be a matter of time till it would be understood that human responsibility is not simply a matter of individual, family, and state, but a matter of life on earth as a whole and, perhaps eventually, even beyond our earth. When that realization combines with the discovery that it is semiosis—the Way of Signs—that leads "everywhere in nature, including [into] those domains where humans have never set foot",[61] a whole new era of ethical understanding dawns. Speculative understanding as the ability to investigate and come to know the subjective constitution and intersubjective connections among things as they exist independently of animal cathexis now expands and extends practical understanding as far as science can turn its knowledge into technology, a development clearly presaged in Aquinas' observation[62] that "speculative understanding by extension becomes practical". And just as the basis of all human understanding, speculative and practical alike, is the action of signs, so the discovery that human control over things extends to a responsibility for the whole of life on earth, including but not restricted to the human, leads to the need for a rethinking of *ethics as stringently bound up with and derived from semiosis*—even as is speculative understanding.

This was a development that first began to be realized in semiotics only as Sebeok's individual life neared its end.[63] Always leery of ideol-

---

[61] Emmeche 1994: 126.

[62] Aquinas 1266: Q. 79, Art. 11, sed contra. This insight Aquinas takes from Aristotle's c.330BC book *On the Soul*. What has changed now—in our day— is only the realization that it is the whole of nature, not just the life of individuals on earth, that is subject to substantial change; whereupon speculative understanding becomes practically limitless in its extension of showing us further how the human animal can introduce into nature fundamental and far reaching changes, touching the heavens themselves—thus demanding an "ethical understanding" not at all confined merely to the realm of human interactions within "society and culture".

[63] Yet here we may also note a curious parallel to the marginal status of Peirce in the original early-to-mid 20th century formation of inquirers into sign as a "community", i.e., as a commonly recognized focus within intellectual culture. As Peirce was marginal to semiotics in its initial phase as semiology, so his entry into the mainstream brought to general attention one of the principal correspondents of his later years, the British Victoria Lady Welby. Welby became known generally, however (outside the Netherlands at least), in the Sebeokean universe of transition from minor to major tradition semiotics mainly, almost exclusively, in terms of her 1903–1911 correspondence with Charles Peirce (see Hardwick 1977), and as coiner (in 1896) of the term "significs".

ogy, Sebeok's seminal work in establishing the experiential basis of semiotics as extending as far as we can prescissively establish an action of signs to be at work in nature indeed is what makes him "belong to the timeless core of semiotics for every period", as Tarasti put it.[64] Without speculative knowledge there is no practical knowledge, only animal cathexis reducing to the self-interest of the organism without regard for "things in themselves". So it must be said that the work of Sebeok's generation was to establish the foundations for our under-

---

In Italy, Welby's emphasis on the "values" or ethical dimension in the action of signs at work among human animals—which is the central meaning of the term "significs"—naturally enough caught the attention of Susan Petrilli, one of Sebeok's main collaborators on the international scene, and this led Sebeok to take an interest in the matter, reflected even in Chapter 13 of his last book (see Sebeok 2001: 145-153). Now, as the 21st century completes its first decade, even as Peirce emerged in from the early 20th century "semiotic sidelines", so we seem destined to witness a similar emergence on the part of his correspondent, Victoria Lady Welby. The first major stage of this emergence, no doubt, is that recorded in the classic turn-of-the-century synchronic survey of semiotics by Ponzio and Petrilli 2005: Chap. 2 "About Welby", 80–137. But this "first glimpse" is as nothing by comparison with the just released volume, Petrilli 2009 *Signifying and Understanding. Reading the Works of Victoria Welby and the Signific Movement*, described by the editor of the series housing the 1,048-page work (Cobley 2009a: ix) as a work exhibiting a "degree of scholarship coupled with theoretical expertise and a vision for the future" that is "seldom to be met with in academic life." He concludes (ibid. x): "If you want to learn how important Welby's writings will be, start with this book." And he is right. (More than that, in my judgment Cobley is the heir to the editorial genius within the semiotic community of Thomas Sebeok himself.)

It is indeed, as Cobley (ibid.) says, Petrilli and not Sebeok who "makes Welby mean much to both the present and the future"; yet this very fact makes equally clear that it will be a long time before the various "moves beyond Sebeok" do not do so while bearing seminal limnings from the work of Sebeok's own lifetime, which more than any other synchronicity of the 20th century established what will be forever more semiotics "major tradition". The main point of Welby's significs (in line with what Sebeok established as the major tradition in semiotics, and similarly to Peirce's approach to the life of signs) is that it transcends pure descriptivism, to study signs and meaning in their ethical, pragmatic and even aesthetic dimensions, where semiotic theory intersects axiology. Thus significs, neatly within the major tradition, moves (or even begins) beyond the strictly epistemological and cognitive boundaries of the sign sciences as first defined semiologically, including specifically those of language and communication studies. Leading beyond the specialism of semantics as proposed in her day, Welby's proposal of significs arises from the assumption that the relation between sign, meaning, and value is of central importance in every possible sphere of human interest and behavior.

standing of semiotics, while success at that huge task in turn made inevitable an "ethical development" of semiotic understanding—the extension of semiotics to encompass also the sphere of human responsibility bound up with and inextricable from anthroposemiosis. Thus "in the 1990s, semiotic research [came] to a kind of parting of the ways", where the main line of development "instigates one to examine *the subject who makes choices*"[65] precisely as bearing responsibility through consciousness of what the "good of the whole" requires over and above yet *also as including* the self-interest of human animals.

The first book to announce this "tipping point" in the development of semiotic consciousness was Eero Tarasti's *Existential Semiotics*, published in 2000, the penultimate year of Sebeok's life and, fittingly enough, as a volume in the "Advances in Semiotics" series that Sebeok edited for the Indiana University Press. The development, long in gestation, was inevitable, needing only a clear and proper name. That name effectively arrived with the publication in 2003 of the book, *Semioetica*, by Augusto Ponzio and Susan Petrilli. Even as Sebeok established semiotics as a global phenomenon within the intellectual culture of the 20th century, so Ponzio and Petrilli properly identified the ethical dimension within global semiotics as *semioethics*[66] — to wit, the attempt

---

[65] Ponzio and Petrilli 2005: 87, italics added. Worth mentioning here as classic among the early semiotic studies of human subjectivity is Colapietro 1989; see also Sebeok 1977a, 1988c, 1989b, and Deely 2010.

[66] As is often, almost normally, the case with decisive terms, this term "semioethics" did not spring simply full blown from the mind of Zeus, but is the outcome of a long series of intellectual reflection. Augusto Ponzio summarized the gestation for me thus in an email of 4 January 2010: "Semioethics was born in early 80s in connection with the introduction to Italian translations by Susan Petrilli of works of Sebeok, Morris, Welby, and my introduction and interpretation of Bakhtin's, Rossi-Landi's, Giovanni Vailati's, and Peirce's works. Our problem was to find a term which indicates study of the relation between signs and values, ancient semeiotica and semiotics .... We coined terms and expressions such as 'teleosemiotica' 'etosemiotica', 'semiotica etica', in contraposition to 'semiotica cognitiva' (see the Italian edition by Bonfantini, *Peirce, Charles Sanders, Semiotics. I fondamenti della semiotica cognitiva* , a cura di Bonfantini et. al.; Torino: Einaudi, 1980). ...

"The beginning of semioethics is in the introductions by me and Susan Petrilli to Italian editions (in translation by Petrilli) of Sebeok, *Il segno e i suoi maestri* (Bari: Adriatica, 1985), and Welby, *Significato, Metafora e interpretazione* (Bari, Adriatica, 1985); in the essays we published in *Essays in Significs*, ed. H. Walter Schmitz (Amsterdam: John Benjamins, 1990); in Susan's books of the 80s such as *Significs, semiotica, significazione* (Pref. by Thomas Sebeok, Adriatica 1988), and my own of that period, such as *Filosofia del linguaggio* (Adriatica 1985).

"In a private note in the context of the International Colloquium

stringently to derive ethics within our understanding of semiosis as the "practical extension" of semiotic consciousness, an inevitable "sequel" thereto, as I have put it.[67]

It was the first move "beyond Sebeok", but a move that became possible only because of Sebeok's central role in shaping the future of the doctrine of signs by exposing the "pars pro toto fallacy" under which 20th century semiotics began, while shifting through that very exposure the foundation of semiotic inquiry from epistemological stipulation à la Saussure to cenoscopic investigation à la Poinsot and Peirce.

'Refractions. Literary Criticism, Philosophy and the Human Sciences in Contemporary Italy of the 1970s and the 1980s', Department of Comparative Literature of Carlton University, Ottawa, 27–19 settembre 1990 (in the discussion of my communication, Rossi-Landi tra 'Ideologie' e 'Scienze umane'), I used the Italian term 'Semioetica', as displacement of 'e' in Italian word 'semeiotica': a play that indicates in Semiotics the ancient vocation of Semeiotics (of Hippocrates and Galen) for improving or bettering life. [See now Petrilli 2007.]

"But in the title of three lessons of Curtin University of Technology in Perth, Australia with Susan I used still 'teleosemiotica': 'Teleosemiotics and global semiotics' (July-September, 1999, Australia, lecture tour: Adelaide University, Monash University of Melbourne, Sydney University, Curtin University of Perth, Northern Territory University of Darwin).

"The book of 2003 by Susan and me, *Semioetica*, is the landing, or final achievement, of this long crossing of texts, conceptions, and words, as it results in bibliographic references."

[67] Deely 2010: "Sequel: the Ethical Entailment of Being a Semiotic Animal", 107–126. See also Deely 2004b, contextualizing the remarks of Petrilli 2004 in the same volume.

Chapter 3

Projecting What We Have Learned about Interdisciplinarity: from 330BC to 2075AD

Becoming conscious of the historicity of human thought with its depth dimension of collective experience, reaching back through generations long dead yet somehow alive now and influencing the unconscious and preconscious development of contemporary minds especially through language as "the House of Being" (in Heidegger's sense),[1] is one of the most essential and humbling dimensions of that metasemiosis we have come to call "semiotics". Therein the semiosis underlying every age of cosmic and biological evolution begins to become conscious of itself in the human being as a semiotic self.

Here, from within the synchronic perspective of 2010, I want to situate this ongoing development of the doctrine of signs as it presents itself to us today precisely as the *inherently interdisciplinary and transdisciplinary perspective and process* in and by which the whole of human knowledge is engendered and organized. Only by becoming conscious of this underlying process—semiosis—do we have the possibility to *best* organize, or at least *better* organize, our institutions and instruments of intellectual culture. As regards its completion, I address now a future task; but its beginning is now, now both as incorporating insights from authors past and as projecting in outline an outcome which will make of interdsciplinarity as semiotics institutionalized within the postmodern academy what specialization as ideoscopic science has been to the modern academy.

For it is high time to resolve the paradox imposed upon us by the modern period of philosophy's long history. The moderns spent almost three centuries trying to persuade one another that the human mind works in such a way that communication cannot occur. This sounds ridiculous, yet communication, presupposed to all argument and discourse, cannot possibly occur if the human mind works the way that Kant, for example, claimed that it did: namely, by forming mental representations behind and beyond which lay the reality of things (including that of other human selves). The development began, no doubt, with Ockham's doctrine that relation has no being of its own

---

[1] See Deely 2000.

other than a mind-dependent being.[2] To take communication seriously, however, is to set out on the road to discovering that not only does relation have a being that can be mind-independent as well as mind-dependent, but that this indifference to the two orders is the *singularity* of relation among all the modes of mind-independent being; for all other varieties of mind-independent being are what they are *only* as mind-independent.

This "singularity" of relation, its positive indifference to circumstance as determining it now to the mind-independent order, now to the mind-dependent order, was used by Aquinas to reconcile the inner life of God as Trinity with the unity of God as *ipsum esse subsistens*. But it was John Poinsot, in 1632, who was the first to latch on to the realization that the singularity of relation is precisely what makes *any and all* communication possible, whether within the Godhead among the Divine Persons, or between God and the world, or within the world between finite creatures of whatever sort. In short, it was Poinsot who first explicitated the point that *relation's singularity is the ground of the prior possibility of semiosis*, and the essence of semiosis wherever an action of signs succeeds to occur.

Thus semiosis effects the interweave between thoughts and things whenever and wherever communication occurs, verbal or otherwise. But why did it take so long for the human animals to realize that they are unique above all in being *semiotic animals*,[3] able to recognize that there are signs and to investigate their action—upon which, it turns out, the whole of animal knowledge, not only that of humans, depends throughout—in contrast to merely using signs, as is true of all animals and even plants and (as it increasingly seems) of the physical environment even in its inorganic aspects of development as first leading up to and afterward sustaining life? The ancients thought of signs only in nature; the Latins took 1100 years to develop their general notion of sign as transcending the nature/culture contrast to the point where it became clear that triadic relations alone complete signs in their proper being; the moderns went adrift entirely, and took almost 300 years to conclude (little else was possible, given the parameters of their so-called epistemology) that there are signs all right, but only in and filtered by culture. Postmodernity began with Peirce's recovery of the line of insight marked out by the premodern Latin development, and

---

[2] See the treatment of Nominalism in Deely 2008.

[3] This notion indeed constitutes a postmodern definition of the human being, one which transcends patriarchy and feminism alike, even as it supersedes the ancient and medieval notion of "rational animal" and (even more) the modern notion of "thinking thing", thanks to semiotics' bridging (as Baenziger remarks on the jacket of Deely 2010) "the chasm of modern philosophy".

so semiotics of the 20th century, though launched with a modern myopia, soon enough (thanks to the later Latins, Peirce, and Sebeok) expanded to its broader horizon of sign-activity throughout nature. But the whole picture, right up to the "postmodernity" of semiotics at the dawn of the 21st century, is clear testimony to Peirce's observation that[4]

> it is extremely difficult to bring our attention to elements of experience which are continually present. For we have nothing in experience with which to contrast them; and without contrast, they cannot excite our attention. ... The result is that roundabout devices have to be resorted to, in order to enable us to perceive what stares us in the face with a glare that, once noticed, becomes almost oppressive with its insistency.

For those who have become reflectively aware of the action of signs, semiosis is as clear as day—oppressively or blindingly clear, as Peirce might say; yet for that as-yet-much-larger multitude who have still to realize the dependency of objects upon signs, and the derivative status of things from objects experienced, "much as a pair of blue spectacles will prevent a man from observing the blue of the sky", so will everyday awareness of objects as "things" prevent one from observing the action of signs underlying all awareness.[5]

Aristotle had a broader conception of psychology than did Saussure. Nonetheless, when he proposed for consideration his famous triangle of mental states, outer things, and utterances communicating between the two,[6] he anticipated Saussure's notion that it was to psy-

---

[4] Peirce 1894: CP 1.134.

[5] Thus semiotics provides the answer to Heidegger's question (1927: 437), "Why does Being get 'conceived' 'proximally' in terms of the present-at-hand and not in terms of the ready-to-hand, which indeed lies closer to us?"— "closer" indeed generically as animals, but not at all closer species-specifically to semiotic animals, at least not once actively engaged analytically in metasemiosis.

[6] Aristotle c.330BC: Περι Ερμηνειασ 16a3–9 (Greek text from Bekker 1831): "Εστι μὲν ουν τὰ ἐν τῇ φωνῇ τῶν ἐν τῇ ψυχῇ παθημάτων σῦμβολα, καὶ τὰ γραφόμενα τῶν ἐν τῇ φωνῇ, καὶ ὥσπερ οὐδὲ γράμματα πᾶσι τὰ αὐτά, οὐδὲ φωναὶ αἱ αὐταί ὧν μέντοι ταῦτα σημεῖα πρώτων, ταῦτα πᾶσι παθήματα τῆς ψυχῆς, καὶ ὧν ταῦτα ὁμοιώματα πράγματα ἤδη ταὐτά. περὶ μὲν οὖν τούτων εἴρηται ἐν τοῖς περὶ ψυχῆς, — ἄλλης γὰρ πραγματείας."
Aristotle *Perihermenias*, 16a3–9, Latin trans. from Boethius c.514AD: "Sunt ergo ea quae sunt in voce earum quae sunt in anima passionum notae, et ea quae scribuntur eorum quae sunt in voce. Et quemadmodum nec litterae omnibus eaedem, sic nec eaedem voces; quorum autem hae primorum notae, eaedem omnibus passiones animae sunt, et quorum hae similitudines, res etiam eaedem. De his quidem dictum est in his quae sunt dicta de anima — alterius est enim negotii."

chology that we should have to look to understand the interweaving of these three elements. Not until the 1632 *Treatise* of Poinsot would we find a full statement to the contrary, a statement to the effect that it is the action of signs, not psychology, that provides the basis for communication by logical or any other means![7]

3.1. Tracing from Within the Present a Long Trajectory

Let us then introduce into our current synchronic view elements from the larger diachrony of our investigation's subject matter, both elements which long antecede our synchrony (from c.330BC), and elements which project beyond the possible duration of our present synchrony (to AD2075 or so). By that time we may reasonably expect that the synchronic conflicts between modern specializations and the need for a cenoscopic framework allowing an overview of ideoscopy within intellectual culture should largely have been resolved—or so we are entitled to hope. Here I can do no more than to lay out some preliminary reflections on this problem of how to "fit semiotics in" to the institutional university structure. After all, it took a couple of centuries for the traditional universities to figure out how to incorporate modern science—i.e., ideoscopic science, the kind of knowledge that could never be arrived at independently of experimentation with instruments extending the senses and mathematization of the results—into their academic structures. Up to the time of Galileo and even a while after, the universities had relied exclusively (but without recognizing its proper nature and limits) on cenoscopy, i.e., the kind of science that semiotics consists in. Within that earlier cenoscopy uncomprehending of cenoscopy's proper limits that was called "Scholasticism", the first establishment of the standpoint required for semiotic (Poinsot 1632)

Aristotle *On Interpretation*, 16a3–9, English trans. from Edghill 1926: "Spoken words are the symbols of mental experience and written words are the symbols of spoken words. Just as all men have not the same writing, so all men have not the same speech sounds, but the mental experiences, which these directly symbolize, are the same for all, as also are those things of which our experiences are the images. This matter has, however, been discussed in my treatise about the soul, for it belongs to an investigation distinct from that which lies before us."

[7] Poinsot 1632: "Remarks on Aristotle's Perihermenias", 38/1–2, and 11–19: "Libri Perihermenias sic vocantur quasi dicas 'de Interpretatione'. ... Sed tamen, quia haec omnia tractantur in his libris per modum interpretationis et significationis, commune siquidem Logicae instrumentum est signum, quo omnia eius instrumenta constant, idcirco visum est in praesenti pro doctrina horum librorum ea tradere, quae ad explicandam naturam et divisiones signorum in Summulis insinuata, huc vero reservata sunt."

came too late to head off the disastrous toppling of ideoscopy from its cenoscopic foundations, a toppling wrought by modern philosophy but precipitated by abuses of cenoscopy in the hands of religious and civil authorities.[8] If we succeed to reinstitutionalize cenoscopy, now *along with* the spectacular ideoscopic achievements of modernity, then we will have performed a great service indeed to the emerging global intellectual culture of the human species. But the success of this enterprise certainly exceeds my synchronic (though not diachronic) participation, and can be expressed in the present pages only after the manner of something like a prognostication. Borrowing Sebeok's words from a similar occasion,[9] and changing only the referent—the *"suppositio"*, as logicians might want to put it—of the opening demonstrative pronoun used adjectivally, I now say that "This abductive assignment becomes, henceforth, the privilege of future generations to pursue, insofar as young people can be induced to heed the advice of their elected medicine men".

This third main section of the present essay intends no more than to provide an "indexical pointer", as it were, an extended index finger indicating a future outcome, to the problem of institutionalizing semiotics within the academic structure of the postmodern university world—or, as we might better put it, the problem of adapting the modern university specializations structure to an intellectual culture no longer modern but postmodern, and hence with no longer only an uncognized semiosis underlying but now also an overlying conscious semiotics at its identifying core.

Let us begin with a backward glance to c.330BC, then proceed by way of prescissive analysis to trace forward to 2075AD or so the trajectory that appears now to have been launched by Aristotle's indication of the fact that an understanding of his words/things/thoughts triangle presupposes "some other science". In the process, we will discover that that "other science", suggested by Aristotle himself as what would develop in the Latin world and continue in the modern world as "psychology", and also "logic" (that one of the three original "liberal arts" concerned with discourse within the soul as the basis for writing and rhetoric alike), turns out to be—that "other science"—neither logic nor psychology, but semiotics.

---

[8] This is the tale I have tried to recount in *The crossroad of signs and ideas* volume with *Descartes & Poinsot* as its main title (Deely 2008), a volume which, fortuitously, was published in the very week that 33rd Annual Meeting of the Semiotic Society of America opened in October of 2008 under the theme of "Specialization, Semiosis, and Semiotics". See now also Deely 2010a.

[9] Sebeok 1984b: 21, in finem.

3.2. The Triangle of Words, Thoughts, and Things

Aristotle's triangle, like all triangles, has three points or "termini" and three sides. The question is, what exactly are the three termini and, in terms of relations, what is represented by the three sides? In English, the three termini may quite accurately be said to be Words, Things, and "Passions of the Soul", which are actually not *thoughts* properly speaking but rather *that upon which the formation of thoughts is based*, or those "specifications" resulting from the physical interaction of the animal's body with the surrounding environment of physical things out of which thoughts grow.

3.3. Pre-Modern Background to Understanding the Triangle

Later, the Latin commentators on Aristotle will develop these points in a terminology which, effectively, was lost in the transition from Latin Age to Modern philosophy.[10] In terms of that (lost) terminology, the *passiones animae* or "passions of the soul" are the forms of specification (*species impressae*) for developing thought which have their origin in the action of sensible things upon the senses, as these stimuli are *further* developed or shaped by the active interpretive response of the internal senses of memory, imagination, and estimation that together or "collectively" constitute, on the side of animal Innenwelt, the foundations or basis (*species expressae*, or "phantasms") for the relations to the environment constituting the animal objective world, the Umwelt.

But these phantasms presenting to the animal its surroundings as interpreted are themselves transformed by the activity of the intellect itself (*intellectus agens*) **from** being *species expressae* as perceptual thoughts **into** being for intellection rather *species impressae*, specificative *passions*—specifying *impressions* passively *received* from the activity of internal sense, serving now not to interpret the outer surroundings, but rather *internally to activate* the *intellectus possibilis* as capable in principle of coming to know "all things", the whole of being.

Thus, what for the brute animal are already thoughts structuring objects perceived, become now for the human animal transformed further into a new level of specificative *passions*. These are specifying impressions actively formed by the activity of internal sense (just as the

---

[10] Maritain (1959: 115 text and notes) terms the species, both impressae and expressae, as being "terms without counterpart in modern philosophy". The reader interested in the full details of the question—actually quite important for semiotics—is referred to the *Intentionality and Semiotics* treatment in Deely 2007b: esp. Chap. 4, "Specifying forms, impressed and expressed – terms without equivalence in modern philosophy", 23–32.

species impressae of external sense are actively formed by the activity of surrounding bodies upon the animal body) but now passively *received* rather from the activity of the intellect transforming the phantasms by adding to them the relation of "self-identity" into a new level of specificative *passions* (i.e., specifying *impressions* passively *received* from the activity of internal sense now "made intelligible").

In this way the phantasms, terminative for the activity of sense, are rendered mediative for the activity of understanding or "intellect". As such, i.e., newly minted as *species impressae intellectus* from the *species expressae phantasiandi*, these "passions of the soul" are not yet impressions from things received via sense *actually* understood, but now at last impressions *able to be thought about intellectually*, and not only as sense-perceived. Only now, in response to *these* "passiones animae" (as "able to be intellectually considered") does the human understanding in its proper and distinctive awareness come to life, responding to the phantasms (the *phantasma transformata*, as it were) in and by the formation of *its own* interpretive specifications of human awareness (*species expressae intellectae*, as opposed to the phantasms transformed into *species impressae intelligibiles*). This final product of intellectual activity, a product not of the *intellectus agens* transforming the phantasms into *species intelligibiles*, but of the *intellectus possibilis* itself (activated by phantasms-as-sense-impressions-now-intelligible) forming on its own *species intellectae* as foundations of relations[11] to objects as they may exist "in themselves" (whether mind-dependently, mind-independently, or in any admixture of the two), constitutes what are commonly termed today "thoughts" or "ideas"—i.e., cognitive in contrast to cathectic psychological states—species-specific to the semiotic animal.

But this modern way of speaking ought not be allowed to blind us to that fact that these species-specifically human thoughts are possible only within and on the basis of the generically animal thoughts which are not species-specific to human animals but are rather generically common to all animals as living in a world of cognized objects irre-

---

[11] I.e., just as the phantasms as *species expressae* of memory, imagination, and estimation are terminative productively but not terminative cognitively, just so the *species expressae* of understanding are terminative productively but as produced serve only and further to provenate relations having objects as their termini. Thus the characteristic of all thought (*species expressae*), generically animal and specifically human equally, as Poinsot best and most clearly put it (1632: Book II, Question 2), is to present what is other than itself, and so to exist and function in the capacity of sign-vehicles; but whereas generically animal thought terminates always and simply at objects as related to the animal, specifically human thought adds to this awareness as self-interested (transforming it without displacing it) the further dimension of awareness of these same objects as involving things in themselves. See Deely 2007b.

ducible to physical things because they are cathectically organized not in the same way that the things are organized but precisely and rather according to the interests and sophistication of the animal perceiving.[12]

3.4. Modern Attempts to Semanticize the Triangle

But we can see even from this brief summary that it is already an "over the top" interpretation of Aristotle's triangle to render the "passions of the soul" without qualification as "thought",[13] and to treat the triangle as fundamentally "semantic", apparently just because it involves "words" as one of its three terms—as we find first in Gomperz (1908), perhaps most famously in Ogden and Richards (1923),[14] and later in the unsound attempts (such as Kretzmann 1967, 1974; esp. O'Callaghan 2003; *inter alia*) to make of this characterization a "Thomistic" interpretation of Aristotle.[15]

Yet it must also be said, in favor of the influential semantic use made of the triangle in that seminal work on meaning by Ogden and Richards, that there are no "words" *until* ideas or concepts have been formed as *incorporative* of the passions of the soul. So we should keep well in mind, while considering this seminal text of Aristotle c.330BC *On Interpretation* 16a3–8, its author's own caveat (italic added): "This matter has, however, been discussed in my treatise about the soul, for

---

[12] The earliest formulation I have found of this insight that will become central to the doctrine of signs in Poinsot's work, to the Umwelttheorie of Jakob von Uexküll, and to contemporary semiotics through and after the work of Sebeok, is in Cajetan 1507: in I.1, art. 3: "aliae enim sunt divisiones entis in esse rei, aliae in genere scibilis" (cited by Poinsot 1632 at 149/44–46).

[13] An attempt to trace the complex origin of the "passions" in the interactions of the human body with surrounding bodies (perhaps in some contradiction with his more general *res cogitans/res extensae* metaphysics) without, however, particular regard to either Aristotle or his triangle, was made in the earliest days of modern philosophy by none other than Descartes himself (1649), in the last of his works to be published in his lifetime.

Interestingly, Descartes' treatment of the "passions" concerns what we would today call cathectic psychological states no less than the cognitive ones. It is a kind of sketch of psychology with an eye to moral philosophy, more relevant to the understanding today of Umwelt theory (in the matter of how the animal organizes its cognized surroundings in terms of objects cathected as +/0/−) than it is to the question of the triangle now before us.

[14] This book, *The Meaning of Meaning*, without doubt made the triangular model much as Aristotle had long ago suggested a central focus in the 20th century semiotics development. See, e.g., "Working with Interpreters of the Meaning of Meaning. International Trends among Twentieth-Century Theorists", Petrilli 2008 or 2010: Essay #2, 49–88.

[15] See details in Deely 2008a.

it belongs to an investigation distinct from that which lies before us". Hence the relevance of the above summary of the Latin commentary tradition on the works of Aristotle, from the time of Albert the Great, the principal teacher of St Thomas Aquinas and the first of the Latins to comment on the full *corpus* of Aristotle's writings, down to the time of Poinsot, who first established the irreducible triadicity of the relational being proper to signs.

3.5. Aristotle's *Caveat* on the Need to Understand the Triangle through "An Investigation Distinct" from Inquiries into Logic and Language

Thus, as we look back on the statement of Aristotle's triangle at the opening of his *Perihermenias* or "On Interpretation" text, we have to note carefully two things: not only that "In these books Aristotle treats principally of the statement and proposition", but also that he opens this treatment by mentioning a triadic structure which, as he himself puts it, "belongs to an investigation distinct" from the matter of spoken and written forms of linguistic communication, a distinct investigation which is not only prior but indeed foundational to the inquiry into logical discourse.

Poinsot, in his own remarks on the text introduced with Aristotle's statement of the triangle, points out that all the matters treated properly and directly in Aristotle's *Books on interpretation* "are treated in those books by way of interpretation and signification, *since indeed the universal instrument of logic is the sign.*"

Then he turns to Aristotle's *caveat*, the matter of the distinct and prior investigation needed to understand the matter of the triangle as it will form part of the discussion, even if not fundamentally, in the "perihermenias books"—the books on the logical component or dimension of interpretation as linguistically expressible.

But here, we shall shortly see, Poinsot goes beyond Aristotle in a rather striking fashion. For Aristotle, the "passions of the soul" belonged primarily and broadly to the treatment of psychology[16]—the *De anima*, which dates from the same period as the *De interpretatione*, indeed, but which Aristotle refers to as "already having been written" when he begins the *De interpretatione*.

3.6. Causality and the Relationships Within and Constitutive of the Triangle

Very important to note from the start, and keep in mind throughout, is the difference between *causal interactions* (Aristotle's categories of

---

[16] Recall Sausure's location of "semiology" as falling under "general psychology".

"action" and "passion") and the *relations* which are generated by and result from those interactions (Aristotle's notion of relation as a *distinct* category of mind-independent being in the very sense that Ockham and modern philosophy after Ockham will relegate exclusively to the status of mind-dependent being). The two are commonly—almost always, historically (which helps to explain the long delay in general establishment of a semiotic consciousness in the long history of cenoscopic science we call "philosophy")—conflated and confused. A causal interaction is commonly called a "causal relation", but this is no more true than it would be to call an offspring a "sexual interaction". Just as a child comes into being through a sexual interaction, but is for sure something distinct from, *over and above*, and subsequently quite independent of that original interaction long since ceased, so it is with relations. Efficient causal interaction (*agere et pati*) requires physical proximity, but not so relations consequent upon physical interaction. "For far or near, a son is in the same way the son of his father";[17] whence "distance neither conduces to nor obstructs the resultance of a pure relation, because these relations do not depend upon a local situation".

3.6.1. Yet action follows upon being: as a thing is, so does it act ("*agere sequitur esse*"); and while the thing acted upon bears the traces of the action upon it, in turn, according to *its* own being ("*quidquid recipitur, secundum modum recipientis recipitur*"), the resulting relation thus necessarily bears the stamp of both action and passion—subject acting and subject acted upon. Thus, in speaking of the *relations* between "things" of the physical environment and "passions" of the soul (that is to say, initially, the *psychological effects* within the animal produced by the interactions within the sphere of awareness of its own body with the surrounding bodies making up its immediate environment), it is not indexicality that Aristotle foregrounds but rather the iconicity that follows upon interaction as indexical, the *formal resemblance* that survives the interaction itself and provides the basis afterwards for tracing even the indexicality—for example, in a forensics investigation.

3.6.2. And it is the same on the other sides of the triangle: Aristotle is focusing on the relations as suprasubjective modes,[18] rather than on

---

[17] Poinsot 1632: Tractatus de Signis, Second Preamble "On Relation", Article 1, "Whether there exist relations which belong to the order of mind-independent being", 85/11–12 and 8–11.

[18] Actually, Aristotle is thinking exclusively in terms of intersubjectivity, as the being relation has in the order of mind-independent τὸ ὄν; only with Poinsot and the formal advent of semiotics will the focus shift to suprasubjectivity as

the causal interactions that relations may involve or presuppose. Psychological states as they issue in vocal sounds, for example, are but creating outward effects *symptomatic* of the inward state. Words as physical sounds or marks (or movements), however symptomatic of inner states, are not thus *words*. As *words* physical sounds, marks, and movements have a *content*, informational or poetic, cognitive or cathectic, more or less pure or mixed, as the case may be; but that *content* depends upon an exaptation, a successful social stipulation and hence (eventually) a *custom*, thanks to which the words refer to the passions and to the things designated as *signified* alike *symbolically* rather than iconically.

3.6.3. Thus, within Aristotle's triangle, the closest we come to indexicality directly considered is in the σημεῖον as symptom[19] relation between "words"—not as such, but as physical occurrences intentionally or unintentionally emitted in the behavior of the human being as an animal organism—and the psychological states or "passions"; whereas the *symbola* relations between words and passions (as also the *symbola* relations between words and things) depend rather upon the superposition or "imposition" of an intention upon those symptoms, whereby they are transformed "conventionally" to become not merely physical occurrences but also linguistic occurrences at the same time. And while as symbols the linguistic occurrences are usually and to a greater or less extent intentional, precisely as *symptoms* they *need not* be intentional. (I may groan in pain merely because of the pain suffered; or I may groan in pain mainly to gain sympathy from those around me—or, of course, both!) So, while passions presuppose indexical interactions with things, these interactions survive in the present mainly as iconic relations. And while words presuppose passions, they do not mainly iconically but rather symbolically represent the content of the passions. Hence only indirectly do words manifest the relation of passions to things, even when they themselves are used directly to speak about things.[20]

---

the being singular to relation as transcending all subjective contrasts within the order of mind-independent being, including the contrast of *ens reale* as including both subjectivity and intersubjectivity to *ens rationis* and purely objective being as ontologically relative throughout, and hence suprasubjective in sign and signified whether or not intersubjective in any given case.

[19] On the general sense of σημεῖον as sign specifically narrowed to σημεῖον as symptom, see Baer 1986.

[20] Poinsot 1632: Tractatus de Signis, Appendix A, 345/9–10 and 349/37–351/8: "Voces unica significatione significant res et conceptus ... principalius [autem] signficent ... res, nisi forte ipsa res significata sit conceptus vel eius intentio.

3.6.4. Yet from this very symptomatic relation of passions to words, arises an adaptive relationship alongside and underlying the exaptive symbolic relation of words to passions; thus secondary features of iconism between passions and words are inevitable intermixtures (entanglements) within the conventional or "arbitrary" relations between words and passions—exactly as Jakobson so late (1965) forced the Saussureans reluctantly to realize. As we will shortly see, Jakobson's point penetrates deeper than even Lotman realized in exposing the inadequacy of the *signifiant/signifié* model as an answer to the guide-

---

"Ratio est, quia ipse conceptus ordinatur ultimate et principaliter ad repraesentandam ipsam rem, cuius est similitudo intentionalis. Ergo vox, quae solum est instrumentum ipsius conceptus in repraesentando et reddit sensibilem [here precisely enters the exaptation transforming Sebeok's "root sense" of language into rather species-specifically human linguistic communication] ipsum conceptum, ad easdem res repraesentandas principalius ordinabitur, quia ad hoc ipsum deservit conceptui. Et licet instrumentum principalius videatur respicere suum principale, a quo movetur, quam effectum, quem facit, tamen hoc intelligitur in ratione operandi et agendi [that is to say, insofar as Secondness is presupposed to and involved within the Thirdness of thoughts as signs—as other-representations]. In ratione tamen repraesentandi, si id quod principale est [in the order of Secondness as causal interaction], etiam est repraesentativum rerum [that is, is other-representative introducing thus Thirdness beyond the self-representation of an effect to its cause in Secondness] et ad ipsam repraesentationem extendendam et manifestandum aliis substituit sibi aliquod instrumentum, praecipium utriusque significatum est res ipsa."

This same cenoscopic point (that words in their application to things reveal ideas only indirectly) Poinsot then expands in the technical terminology I have pointed out (following Maritain—see Deely 2007b). It is an important point (though it disappears from the discourse of modern philosophy), because it clarifies the difference between the direct causality of Secondness and the indirect causality of Thirdness as semiosis (ibid. 351/14–40): "si dicas ... conceptus seu verbum [interior] non significant principaliter res expressas, sed suum principium exprimens ... ergo etiam verbum exterius principalius repraesentabit suum principium, scilicet conceptum, quam rem significatam et expressam, respondetur conceptum seu verbum esse expressionem sui principii formalis, quod est species impressa fecundans intellectum exprimentem, et haec repraesentat obiectum, cuius formaliter est species, et sic conceptus repraesentando suum principium formale repraesentat principaliter suum obiectum formale. Creaturae autem sunt obiectum secundarium et materiale, et ideo non principaliter repraesentatur a Verbo Divino. Unde non sequitur, quod verbum exterius repraesentet principalius conceptum, quia non est formale obiectum repraesentatum, sed principale significativum. Praeterquam quod vox non est naturalis expressio sui principii sicut conceptus, sed imposita et directa ad significandum id, quod conceptus."

question of semiotics: what is the being proper to and distinctive of sign? For dyads do not a triad make, however much Thirdness depends upon Secondness in multiple ways. What Lotman (1990: 6) considered to be the 'unrejectable cornerstones' of modern semiotics prove not rather to be so much *rejectable* as *definitively regional* abstractions necessary to create the analytical fiction of *langue* as a purely synchronic "essence" not only "external to the individual" but further something the individual "by himself is powerless either to create or to modify".

3.6.5. Ah yes, but insofar as this *langue* "exists only in virtue of a kind of contract agreed between the members of a community",[21] while the individual "by himself" is powerless to create or to modify it, that same individual as a semiotic animal, even though happening to be a member of that "contractually bound community", can indeed and often enough *does* succeed to modify the *langue* from without. This possibility of success obtains precisely because linguistic communication *is not* the primary but only the *secondary* modeling system within anthroposemiosis, exactly as Sebeok was the first to point out[22] in his ingenious synthesizing of the work of von Uexküll and Lotman[23] into a single vision of anthroposemiosis as not only a species-specific process but also always and essentially a generically animal process as well.[24] *Within*

---

[21] Lotman 1990: 5.

[22] See Sebeok 1984a, 1987, 1988, 1989a, 1991a, 1991b, 1998.

[23] See the Appendix to the present work, "Sebeok's Synthesis: the Tartu-Bloomington-Copenhagen School", p. 95ff.; and pp. 30-31 above.

[24] The point of Sebeok's synthesis is that any exclusive focus on language, whether in the root sense of the species-specifically human adaptation within the Innenwelt as generically animal, or in the sense of linguistic communication as an exaptation of that biologically underdetermined adaptive feature, distorts the place in nature and biosphere as a whole of the human as animal. Such a focus—precisely the focus of "semiology" as originally conceived to be the whole of the "new science of signs"—distortively glosses over generically zoösemiosis both as regards the dependency of language in its root sense upon those larger processes and as regards the overlap thereof within anthroposemiosis. For it is the zoösemioses with which anthroposemiosis is intertwined and interdependent even for the exercise of its species-specific communication as linguistic that constitutes that "primary modeling process" as a whole on the basis of which the biologically underdetermined feature of "language in the root sense" becomes accessible for exaptation in the first place.

At the Innenwelt level, "language" is anything but an independent feature: language in this root and at that level is precisely that—a feature within the larger whole of an animal modeling system, just as is any species-specific Innenwelt adaptation of the animal modeling system as giving rise to com-

anthroposemiosis overlapping zoösemiosis, then, "linguistic communication" arises as *an exaptation* rather than an adaptation. Saussurean *langue*, we may say, is but the abstract model of that biologically underdeveloped feature of the human Innenwelt which, as exapted, created in the first place linguistic communication as the species-specifically human system indispensable for entry, beyond "society", into the realm of culture as constituting finally the tertiary modeling system.

3.6.6. Synchrony in a near-geometic sense may be the essence of Saussurean *langue* as a secondary modeling system, but diachrony is the essence of language in the root sense from which *langue* is exapted. And precisely from the biologically undetermined human Innenwelt still generically animal come those changes "only in one or other of its elements" [i.e., the elements of *langue*] which are initially "outside the system" of *langue*, indeed, while it remains that "the systems [within *langue*] are affected by them". Here already is decisive proof that synchrony, the essence of *langue* as a secondary modeling system, can *only as an abstraction* (comparable to the abstraction by which Euclidean geometry was achieved) even partially escape diachrony as a larger context within which evolution—cosmic, biological, linguistic—is inevitable, and from which *signifié* in the semiotic sense (*significatum*), in sharp contrast to the semiological sense of *signifié* (mental representation), cannot be omitted.[25]

3.7. Brief Excursus on "Deconstruction"

Consider. In Aristotle's triangle, as we are about to see, on side #1 (the base),[26] words and things are directly connected only unilaterally, in a one-sided and 100% symbolic relation directly *from* the words *to* the things. There is no mutual relation, no *direct* relation back from the things to the words. To speak of, there is no iconicity, no indexicality. There is the direct relation through stipulation (and, after, custom) from words to

---

municative channels distinctive of this or that group of animal individuals. Details of Sebeok's argument are laid out in Deely 2007.

[25] Broden (2009: 20–21) puts it this way: Saussure's "*Course in General Linguistics* seems to exaggerate the extent to which linguistics and its object of study can be defined as one, homogeneous, and neatly bounded and situated. The efforts deployed to this end effectively isolate language and its study from the rest of the social and natural world. ... Similarly, while it founds its central 'mechanism of language' on fundamental cognitive processes, the essay describes both thought and sound as 'amorphous' before language as social convention constitutes each, thereby slighting the incidence of other sensory-motor processes and of mimetic learning."

[26] Section 3.8.1. p. 70 below.

things whereby the words are symbols, that is all; but there is no direct relation from the things back to the words. Here alone, we will see, could one have a chance to speak of something like "arbitrariness" with little or no entanglement of iconicity, "pure" arbitrariness. But not only does Saussure not look to this relation in his linguistic sign-model, he makes no direct place for it in the model, no place at all.

On side #2 of the triangle (things to thoughts),[27] there is a direct, two-way relation between thoughts (as "passions of the soul") and things, indeed; but this iconic, reciprocal relation has *no direct connection with words*.

On side #3 of the triangle[28] (thoughts to words, words to thoughts), there is no single two-way relation between thoughts and words, *nor is there a single one-way relation between thoughts and words*. What there is on this side are *two* one-way relations, one of thoughts to *words as symptoms* of mental representations (passions to vocal, gestured, or written expressions), and a second of words to *thoughts as symbolized* (linguistic expressions to passions).

So, if we consider the relations in which *words alone* are *directly related* to anything other than themselves, we see that there are three such relations: 1st) there is a relation of words to things, which is a symbolic relation, "arbitrary" in the sense of wanting for any internal iconicity or indexicality; 2nd) there is a relation of words to thoughts inasmuch as the words symbolize the thoughts, a relation which is also arbitrary as wanting internal iconicity or indexicality directly yet not without *entanglement* therein; and 3rd) there is a relation of words to thoughts as *symptoms* (σημεῖα) thereof, which relation involves *both* indexicality *and* iconicity.

In Saussure's arbitrary *signifiant/signifié* model, not only is side #3 of the triangle *the only side* taken into consideration, but within that side *only the second* of the *two distinct* one-way relations, the purely symbolic one, not the one of mixed iconicity and indexicality (the σημεῖα relationship) entangled with the symbolic relation.

So when Saussure says that the elements of linguistic communication are *arbitrary*, this is true concerning two of the three relations in which words are directly involved, but, of these *two* "arbitrary" relations of words, *only one*, the symbolic relation of words to thoughts, is considered and incorporated into the *signifiant/signifié* model, the *patron général*. Jakobson and Lotman will, in effect, object that the *non-arbitrary* σημεῖον relation cannot be simply excluded from the *patron général*, because the "arbitrariness" of the *signifiant* to the *signifié* relation is irreducibly and inescapably entangled[29] with the iconic/indexical status of words as σημεῖα.

---

[27] Section 3.8.2, p. 74 below.

[28] Section 3.8.3, p. 76 below.

[29] See note 12 of Section 2.2, pp. 26-29 above.

Now, if we combine the "fact" of the twofold arbitrariness of words with the further "fact" of entanglement wherein "arbitrary" words as σύμβολα of thoughts are *at the same time inextricably as well* σημεῖα of these same thoughts, whence, inescapably, iconic and indexical elements that can be neither stipulatively controlled nor reduced to symbolicity enter into the *signifiant/signifié* "arbitrariness", we have the basis for the prior possibility of what becomes, in the semiological work of Jacques Derrida, the project of "deconstruction". Objects signified (i.e., significates in the semiotic sense, which *need not be and usually are not* mental representations)[30] are omitted from the Saussurean model, wherein the *signifié* is *never anything but a mental representation* in interplay iconically with other mental representations within the subjectivity of the user of *langue*.

Deconstruction is a project to which any and every text is thus (indeed!) a-priori liable. But, what needs to be noted—and what seems constantly to escape the notice of deconstructionist Derridean epigones — is that the ultimate source of the passions in the environmental interaction (both cultural and physical) of human animals with material surroundings objectified in turn imposes *indirect limits* on the deconstructive process,[31] just as more *directly* there is also need for consideration at times (though far from always, and deconstruction as a method marks a great advance in the understanding of this matter) of the "intentions of the author". (Deconstruction as a process normally tends legitimately and systematically to leave out of consideration authorial intention as a factor in the construal of texts. Yet there are times when such intention as textual factor cannot be omitted from consideration without some distortion of sense at critical junctures, so far as linguistic signs have not only a customary and iconic dimension but also and always a stipulative dimension as well, which is exactly what separates them within the class of "customary signs" from the purely customary signs of the "brute" animals overlapping within the semioses of human animals, and conversely.)

Thus the omission in semiology (i.e., in the Saussurean model proposed for sign-in-general) of a *signifié* in the semiotic sense of significate or "object signified",[32] which results in the complete elimina-

---

[30] The exception is the case of self-reflexion in a semiotic animal: see Poinsot 1632: Appendix A, The Signification of Language, "On the relations between words, ideas, and objects", 342-351, esp. 349/37–351/14 (focused below at note 73).

[31] This is also discussed in Eco 1990, esp. Chap. 1.

[32] And, as I have elsewhere noted (Deely 2009c, d, e, f, g, h), the "signified" in the expression "object signified" is tacitly redundant, made necessary only by sedimentation into late-modern national-language usage of the Cartesian

tion of the consideration of things-as-they-are-in-themselves from the theoretical ambit of semiological analysis, is exactly what leads (not necessarily, but in the practice of thinkers mistakenly thinking that the Saussurean dyadic sign-conception is indeed a *general* model, which it is not) to the abusive and narcissistic excesses of deconstruction (mis)construed and (mis)applied as a "universal method of linguistic and cultural analysis". This same blunder, expressed in several issues of the *History and Theory* journal over the last two decades, can be seen as the root of the dilemma in which some contemporary historians— falsely thinking that semiology as such is "postmodern"[33]—find themselves unable to explain the difference between historiography and fiction.[34] This again is a logical consequence of failing to recognize the duplicity of the notion of *signifié* hidden (or lost) in the dyadicity of the Saussurean proposal for the being proper to "sign".

A valuable method and landmark contribution to the development of semiotic consciousness, deconstruction is but a tool among others for achieving textual interpretation, distortive however when it is (mis)taken for or (mis)represented as the "whole story"[35] (or even "last word") in the reading of texts. Deconstruction provides but a prelimi-

---

reversal of the subject/object distinction as it had been developing toward thematic expression in the later Latin centuries, a reversal wherein "subject" acquired a dominant sense of "psychological" and object a dominant sense of synonymy with "thing"—in contrast to the semiotic sense where "object" means always the second of three terms under a triadic relation, whether or not the object also has a subjective existence along with its objectivity, and "subject" means always an individual unit here-and-now part of the physical universe.

[33] On the question of postmodernity falsely so-called, see Deely 2001: 611, text with notes 1 and 2, and the whole of Chap. 16; cf. also Deely 1986 for a perspective on semiology as a sub-development within semiotics more generally as the doctrine of signs.

[34] By far the most extensive treatment of the traditional "history discipline" in relation to semiotics, including this "contemporary" historiographical problem, is to be found in the writings of Williams Deely, beginning as early as 1982. A collected volume of these writings is in preparation as a volume in the Mouton de Gruyter "Semiotics, Communication and Cognition" series (SCC) under the general editorship of Paul Cobley with Kalevi Kull.

[35] Exactly as when the Saussurean dyadic code model for sign is represented as "the whole story" of semiotics. In such cases, at this point in history, what started out as a "pars pro toto fallacy"—the idea that the cultural sphere of sign action is the whole sphere of sign action, the original claim of "semiology"—molts into a "pars pro toto fraud", when an exclusively semiological approach to signs (mis)represents itself as semiotics without qualification, as in Chandler 2002. See gloss thereon in References.

nary step, more -or-less useful depending upon how rigid the reading of a given text has become or is tending to become (as, for example—to take an illustration at the utmost extreme[36]—in the view of some Muslim 'believers' that Koranic texts are not subject to interpretation, and so cannot be translated into another language: the original or nothing![37]).

3.8. The Relationships Within and Constitutive of the Triangle

If we look at Aristotle's triangle now in this light, having as its three terms Words, Passions of the Soul (principally *species impressae* strictly, but also and secondarily *species expressae* as both source and indirect significate of words), and Things, and viewing those terms against the background of the various causalities from which relationships arise in the first place, what do we find are the *relationships* that make up the sides of this triangle? What are the relationships that obtain among the terms of this triangular structure?

The question is not as simple as one might imagine, or as is usually supposed in the literature that has grown up around this triangle (in which literature, as far as I know, the *actual* relationships embodied in the three sides have never been scrutinized in detail). For analytical purposes let us label the base side of the triangle, between *words* and *things*, #**1**; then the side of the triangle from *things* to *passions* #**2**; and the side of the triangle between *passions* and *words* #**3**.

The choice behind this numbering is not simply arbitrary, but is based on the consideration of increasing relational complexity as we move around the three sides.

Triangle side #1 is the relationally simplest of the three: it involves only one single relation of symbolicity, and that one single relation is, moreover, univalent, obtaining only from the side of words as *fundamenta* to things as *termini* of a symbolic relation that has no component besides itself to make it anything other than "arbitrary", "conventional", or (most basically) "stipulated".

Triangle side #2 is likewise simple in involving but a single relation, this time of iconicity rather than symbolicity; but this one single

---

[36] There are similar controversies along this line, but back in the 16th and 17th centuries, over the translation of the Bible.

[37] But of course, were it true that the Koran "cannot be interpreted", then it could not be read either or understood in any language, including its "original Arabic". For there are sounds but no words without involvement of concepts, and concepts differ from sensations precisely in being interpretations, *species expressae*, as we saw in Section 3.3, pp. 56-58 above. To have a thought is to have an interpretation of that thought's object, be it also a thing or 'purely objective'—as in the case of a book 'not subject to interpretation', or a square circle, etc.!

relation is bivalent rather than univalent: the iconicity relation constitutive of this side of Aristotle's triangle obtains equally when we look
from things to passions and when we look from passions to things.

Triangle side #3 is the side that is most complex relationally. It does
not involve one single relation, but two relations, neither of which is
bivalent and each of which is univalent, but in opposite directions.
When we look from the words to the passions, exactly as when we look
from the words to the things, we find only one single univalent relation
of symbolicity. But unlike the univalent symbolic relation of words to
things, the univalent symbolic relation of words to passions as constituting this side of the triangle does indeed have another component
besides itself which interferes with the "purity" of its symbolicity, and
hence, as we will see, with the propriety of labeling it simply "arbitrary" in whatever sense of that word we care to choose. For *in order to
be symbols*, and not merely physical marks or sounds or movements,
the symbolic relation between words and things presupposes a *symptomatic* relation between the words and the passions. *This* relation,
obtaining when the "words" are looked at from the side of the passions
as symbolized, imports into the words indirectly, or "secondarily", as
Jakobson puts it, precisely elements of the iconicity in the passions and
ideas deriving from them that environmental things introduce into the
awareness of animal organisms in the interaction between the animal
bodies and the bodies surrounding the animal bodies.

In order to appreciate the relevance of Aristotle's triangle to the doctrine of signs, bear in mind that the question of the being proper to
relations, the *singularity* of the indifference of relation to all the subjective divisions of being which makes semiosis in the first place possible
at all, is undoubtedly the *ground-question* of semiotics. The *guide-question*
is rather the question of the relational being itself of signs as involving
irreducibly three terms in any fulfillment of semiosis as the action consequent upon that being, and consider that two of the three terms of
Aristotle's triangle are actual signs (words as words and passions as
thought), while the third term, things, are as potential objects products
(significates) precisely of the action of signs, able to become, moreover,
signs in their own right as well as objects. With these two considerations
in mind, the relevance of Aristotle's triangle to the doctrine of signs, if
not (as we will see) the triangular imagery or representation itself, is
undeniable. It is this relevance that we want precisely to identify in the
elements provided by each of the three sides of this triangle—this, as we
will see, *presemiotic triangle*—so often mislabeled as rather (I have com-
mitted this error myself on previous occasions) a "semiotic triangle" or
"semantic triangle" or "triangle of meaning".

Let us, then, examine each of the sides in turn, to see exactly what
of relation they involve.

3.8.1. *The triangle side #1 between words and things.* Looking at the side of the triangle representing a relation between words and things, the most striking feature is the *poverty* of the relationship which constitutes this "side". The relationship is purely one-sided, one-way, and exclusively symbolic, as close to empty of indexicality and iconicity as could be. Whatever there is of indexicality depends wholly on the will or "intention" of the speaker, his or her freedom to *stipulate*, Alice-in-Wonderland fashion.[38] Whatever there is of iconicity is twice-removed from the things objectified, i.e., the things as spoken about, derivative exclusively and indirectly from the "passions of the soul", and only thence, if at all—"twice-removed", as has been said—from the objectified things (through their more direct influence on the passions in the interaction of the animal body with its physical surroundings). Thus, while there is a relation of words to things, there is no direct relation at all back from things to the words discussing or "naming" them.[39] And the one-sided relation of words to things, with no *direct* relation at all back (from the *things* spoken about to the words spoken), is simply that of convention and culture, a matter of σύμ-βολον—nothing more, nothing less, nothing besides.

3.8.1.1. But of course the "things as things" are never quite wholly even when partially the same as the "things as objects"; and while the things spoken about as things are normally wholly independent of the words used to speak about, denote, refer to, or name (actually: *to signify*) them, the things as objects have no such total independence, so that even on this side of the triangle "the conventional dimension of languages", as Broden points out,[40] can be said to "represent 'genuine

---

[38] "When I use a word", Humpty Dumpty said, in a rather scornful tone, "it means just what I choose it to mean, neither more nor less".

"The question is", said Alice, "whether you can make words mean so many different things".

"The question is", said Humpty Dumpty, "which is to be master—that's all".

[39] And here it is worth recalling Augustine's profound point that all words, as items of linguistic communication, be they nouns or verbs, pronouns or adjectives, categorematic or syncategorematic—all items of linguistic communication taken in their distinctive and proper being are names.

[40] Broden 2009: 15, which echoes Saussure i.1907–1911: in the Baskin trans. p. 76. Poinsot, approaching this matter from the side of "ideas" as so-called "formal signs" (that is, psychological states which signify whether or not they are themselves objectified) rather than from the side of "words" as "instrumental signs" (that is, material realities of the physical surroundings which must be themselves objects of awareness in order to function also as signs), nonetheless echoes the point made much more straightforwardly by Saussure and Broden: see *Tractatus de Signis* Book III, Question 4, on the

institutions'" definitely constraining the Alice-in-Wonderland sense of "arbitrariness". In short (ibid.), *stipulation* as a matter of individual will is never the whole story, even on this weakest side of the triangle: even here, "arbitrary" means "fixed at a moment in history through their use [i.e., the use of linguistic signs, words] by a given community", even though "ever subject to change in the process of their transmission through time and individual speakers."

3.8.1.2. Nonetheless, when Saussure speaks of language as the *patron général* for a science of signs and identifies the signs of language as "arbitrary", the "common sense" response of the unsophisticated reader or listener is to think precisely of this relation of words to things as the paradigm of arbitrariness in the sign/signified model. But of course, in thinking thus, "common sense" as usual (or at least all too often) leads directly to a theoretical disaster. For not only is Saussure *not* thinking of the relation of words to things as signifieds, but there is also in fact no **direct** *place in his system of langue* which includes objects in the sense according to which they can be partially identified with things existing independently of thought. That is to say, the Saussurean model of sign has no place for the *object signified*, but only for the idea or "thought" which words in their common usage seldom signify directly at all outside the specialized discourses of philosophy, psychology, and some social sciences,[41] *on the basis of which* objects are signified and also things become objects.

3.8.1.3. For once it is understood that the difference between a sign and an object lies in the difference between self-representation and *other*-representation, it becomes possible to understand the formula that Peirce took from the Conimbricenses, that "all thought is in signs"—because that is precisely what thought consists in (the representation of what is *other* than the thought itself, namely, its object, whether that object is also a thing independent of thought or not).

"Distinctio inter conceptum ultimatum et nonultimatum", 334/1–340/4. See note 51 below.

The weakness in this aspect of Poinsot's semiotic analysis appears precisely in the hindsight of our understanding of language as a secondary modeling system in the shaping of individual identity. Broden (2009: 27) well states the situation as it appears to us today: "From the foundational I-thou relation spring both speech and the subject; language no longer appears as an external instrument of communication which the individual freely manipulates, but rather as the symbolic and dialogic dimension in which subjectivity and especially intersubjectivity are constituted."

[41] See the text from Poinsot 1632: *Tractatus de Signis*, Appendix A, 345/9–10 and 349/37–351/8, cited in note 20 above on p. 61-62.

Things objectified represent themselves in awareness, but they do so only on the basis of the other-representations presenting things in awareness, thoughts as signs. When in turn objects signified become themselves signs, they no longer represent only themselves but *something else* as well. Thus, whether the vehicle of signification, the "sign" in the sense of some individual or aspect thereof, is first of all a material object or first of all a psychological state, in both cases it is the element of *other*-representation that makes the sign be a sign. And this represented other is presented to or for some third—the animal perceiving, for example: hence the triadic character of the sign-relation in every actual semiosis.

3.8.1.4. "Common sense" might suggest that this words-things "side" of Aristotle's triangle would best have constituted Saussure's model of the *patron général* for his (false) idea that a "science of signs" can be constructed on the foundation of the "arbitrariness" of linguistic signs. Thinking in this "common sense" way, however, quite misses Saussure's objective abstractly to constitute *langue* as a system (a geometrical synchrony) complete unto itself, "self-contained", as it were (and is likely to miss as well Saussure's central insight in finding a way, as Broden puts it,[42] to describe language "holistically as a *system* constituted by *relations*"). We can see from Aristotle's triangle that indeed words considered as "*signifiants*" are "arbitrary"—arbitrary in relating as *symbola* to their *signifiés*, and this is so whether we take the *signifié* to be the passions (Saussure's own taking) or whether we take the *signifié* to be the things objectified "about which" the words are spoken, as do the more "naive" interpreters of Saussure relying over-much on "common sense".

3.8.1.5. But we can also see that this "arbitrary" relation of Saussure's model, whether on the misled "common sense" taking or on Saussure's own theoretical taking, presupposes rather than includes a "missing third". On the common sense mistaking, it is the interpretant (in this case a mental representation, the "concept" or "idea") that is missing. But on the Saussurean theoretical taking, what drops out of the *signifiant/signifié* is rather the objectifiable things as things that language can be and normally is used to speak of.[43]

---

[42] Broden 2009: 11.

[43] And indeed they are no part of linguistics on any accounting, but rather the concern of the ideoscopic "hard sciences", including biology, where, however, in zoösemiosis, as semiotics has made unmistakable, linguistic communication finds itself in an unavoidable overlap with nonlinguistic channels of animal communication.

3.8.1.6. Yet there remains the fact, even in the theoretical taking of Saussure, as we will see when we come to examine the third side of the triangle (the words/passions side), that words are symptomatic *index-ically* of passions *iconically* related to the very "things" to which the words themselves lack both symptomaticity and indexicality as direct-ly necessary elements (and which Saussure hence omits from his model). Only when is added, however, the nonarbitrary but indirect yet indexical/iconic connection of words to things *via* the passions as caused by the action of things, only then do the words *fully* exist as signs *actually* signifying in direct speech—so that, as Poinsot put it in his original establishment of the sign as triadic,[44] not dyadic:

> Only when the mind is considered as a term attained by the word indirectly do we see that the significate attained by the word directly is involved as sign in one single relation of three terms [that is to say, in an irreducibly *triadic* relation], *which relation alone constitutes the proper and formal being of the sign* as sign.

3.8.1.7. In other words, in actual speech, in "ordinary language", the *signifié* is an object signified, a "*significatum*", in precisely the sense

---

[44] Poinsot 1632: *Tractatus de Signis* Book I, Question 3, 154/5–30: "Ut ergo non solum pure obiective, sed etiam significative respiciat potentiam, inquiren-dum restat, an illamet relatio, qua significatum respicit, et in ordine ad quod rationem signi induit, illamet etiam respiciat potentiam, cui signatum hoc manifestandum est a signo; an vero relationem habeat ad signatum purifi-catam et absolutam a respectu ad potentiam, alia vero relatione respiciat potentiam in ratione obiecti, et utraque concurrat ad rationem signi con-stituendam, vel etiam in ipsa ratione signi praeter rationem obiecti reperiatur duplex relatio, altera ad potentiam, altera ad signatum.

"Et consurgit difficultatis ratio, quia ex una parte signum non respicit solum signatum in se, sed in ordine ad potentiam, cum in definitione signi ordo ad potentiam includatur, scilicet quod sit manifestativum potentiae etc. Si ergo ratio signi respectum istum dicit ad potentiam, vel unica et eadem relatione respicit utrumque, et currunt difficultates infra attingendae, quia sunt termi-ni omnino diversi, cum respectu potentiae sit solum relatio rationis: respectu signati sit ordo mensurati ad mensuram, respectu potentiae e contra potentia sit mensurabilis ab ipso signo ut ab obiecto cognito. Vel est diversa relatio signi ad potentiam et signatum, et sic non erit signum in praedicamento rela-tionis, quia in ratione signi non est unica relatio, sed pluralitas relationum.

Sit nihilominus conclusio: Si potentia et signatum considerentur ut termini directe attacti per relationem, necessario exigunt duplicem relationem in signo, sed hoc modo signum respicit potentiam directe ut obiectum, non for-maliter ut signum. Si vero consideretur potentia ut terminus in obliquo attactus, *sic unica relatione signi attingitur signatum et potentia, et haec est propria et formalis ratio signi*" (italic added).

left unconsidered in the terms of Saussure's model, and only indirectly or secondarily is the *signifié* the psychological state of the language user, as Saussure postulates for the direct and restricted purposes of his system.[45] We shall return to this point when we reach an examination the third side of the triangle, where we will be able to identify the root of the "debate", as Lotman calls it, between Saussure and Jakobson.

3.8.2. The triangle side #2 between things and passions. We turn now to the second side of our triangle, the side representing the relationship between things of the world and passions of the soul. This side is in a way, if not the simplest, at least the most straightforward of the three sides. It involves a relation that is single but bi-lateral, thus perfectly symmetrical, in contrast to the single relation between words and things which is unilateral and hence asymmetrical. Things are related to passions of the soul most fundamentally in exactly the way that passions of the soul are most fundamentally related to things of the world: as ὁμοιώματα—"likenesses". *Agere facit simile sibi:* an agent stamps its likeness on its effects. Thus are the "passions" and the things as producing them likenesses of one another, reciprocal likenesses, indexically constituted from interactions between animal organism and physical surroundings, the passions related as iconic effects of the things as causes[46] brought about by the interaction of the animal body (be the animal human and semiotic or brute and semiosic only) with the surrounding bodies of its immediate environment.

---

[45] "Following Bréal," Broden notes (2009: 11, citing Saussure i.1907–1911: 99–100, with cross-references) "a natural language and the human 'linguistic faculty' that informs it represent not an external object but a cognitive phenomenon for a subject: 'Synchronic linguistics will be concerned with the logical and psychological relations that bind together coexisting terms and form a system in the collective mind of speakers'."

[46] We can see from this consideration how Boethius' choice of one Latin term— *nota*, a synonym of *signum* but with the connotation of an "index", closer to ὁμοιώματα and σημεῖα as 'symptoms' than to σύμβολα—to designate *all three* sides of Aristotle's triangle, whereas Aristotle himself had used σημεῖα both narrowly (in the sense of symptom) and for only *one* relation on *one* side of the triangle (see Boethius' text in note 6, p. 53 above), threw Pedro da Fonseca into a fit when he read Aristotle's own Greek text for himself, rather than through the eyes of the earlier Latins ignorant of Greek who had relied upon perforce the rendering of Boethius. It was one of the most dramatic moments in the whole Latin development of semiotics, one which had a shaping influence on Descartes' college years and in its own time threatened to derail the Latin discussion of sign as it had developed independently of ancient Greek philosophy in the Latin centuries after Augustine and Boethius. See Deely 2001: Chapter 9, "Three outcomes, two destinies", 411–446. See also Deely 2010a: Chapters 9-12.

3.8.2.1. Precisely here does the fuller treatment of the *De anima* that Aristotle refers to enter in to the consideration of his triangle. While practically everyone in philosophy today, across the schools, is in agreement that philosophy is about "experience" above all, it was not so in ancient Greek and medieval Latin times. Ancient and medieval philosophy took as the primary concern the reality independent of experience, not experience as involving an interweave of mind-dependent and mind-independent being; and of experience itself they had an exceedingly narrow view, amounting to little more than Aquinas' definition of sensation as "actio sensibilis in sensu"—the action of the sensible thing upon the sense organs of the animal body.[47]

3.8.2.2. Thus, when Aristotle spoke of the "passions of the soul", he had in mind primarily *both* the beginnings of animal awareness (or "knowledge") *and* the constant tie-in of that knowledge to the sensible world of interacting things—albeit among human animals (as we saw in Section 3.3., p. 56ff. above) as that chain of "ties to sensation" is the initial point of departure in understanding for the formation of properly intellectual concepts (or *species expressae intellectae* in contrast to the *species impressae intelligibiles*), which are themselves tied to the *species impressae sentiendi* via the *species expressae phantasiandi* or "phantasms" without which there could be no human knowledge at all.

3.8.2.3. "Sensatio est actio sensibilis in sensu"—"sensation is the action of a material object upon the animal body's organ of sense": this action belongs to the order of brute Secondness as a dyadic interaction; but because *agens facit simile sibi*, because an agent produces an effect in the likeness of its being as acting, the resulting relation which survives the dyadic interaction of "cause and effect" (or "agent and patient") is necessarily and irreducibly an iconic relation, even as bespeaking or revealing (through iconicity) the indexicality of its origin.

3.8.2.4. Again, we are dealing with an aspect of the ancient triangle

---

[47] "Realism", for the ancients and medievals, had a much narrower focus than what that term evokes in modern and postmodern philosophy (see Deely 1992, the tenth reading in Cobley Ed. 2009a, for details; consult also relevant essays in Cobley Ed. 2009). The term connoted and denoted purely and simply the role of the senses in knowledge. And indeed, true to the medieval heritage, this focus corresponded exactly to the manner in which experience was defined, both in the Thomistic line and among the Latins generally, as writers of the period testified (see, for example, the authoritative summary of Poinsot 1632: 306/13–307/4, in which the physical presence of a thing acting upon an external sense organ is described as "the paradigm case of experience"—"est ipsamet experientia"). See Deely 1992.

that is crucial for the understanding of semiotics (omitted from the *signifiant/signifié* model, nonetheless), inasmuch as sensation (even as prescissively prior to the formation of those other-representations or "concepts" by which *all animals* evaluate what of their physical surroundings they become aware of in sensation) is already a semiosis. As such, it involves from its first moment and throughout triadic sign relations whereby, in this case, the common sensibles on the basis of the proper sensibles make the animal aware of its surroundings (sights, sounds, smells, shapes, movements, positions, etc.) as in need of evaluation for purposes of the sensing organism's well-being an survival.[48]

3.8.3. *The triangle side #3 between passions and words.* The relation between passions and words turns out to be not one but two quite different relations depending upon which way we look at. It also turns out to be the *only* side that is given consideration in Saussure's *signifiant/signifié* model, upon which he vainly thought to found a complete "science of signs". But let us focus on the relations constitutive of this side.

3.8.3.1. Looked at one way, words must be said to appear as and to be σημεῖα, not in the general sense of "signs" but in the specific ancient sense of "symptoms"—to wit, symptoms of the presence of thoughts, as certain red marks on the skin manifest the underlying presence of the viral disease measles, etc. But, at the same time, properly and in their own right as linguistic media of communication, words for

---

[48] Poinsot 1632: *Tractatus de Signis*, Book I, Question 6, 204/9–11 and 205/34–37: "Bruta proprie utuntur signis, tam naturalibus quam ex consuetudine"; et "non solum sensus interni, sed etiam externi in nobis et in brutis percipiunt significationem et utuntur signis." The theoretical importance of this point has perhaps been best stated by another cryptosemiotician, in this case Josephus Gredt (1924: iv): "Scripto nostro tamquam unica via ad idealismum vitandum manifestatur realismus naturalis integralis philosophiae thomisticae, cujus cardo in doctrina consistit de sensuum externorum cognitione intuitiva excludente quamcumque speciem expressam." But this implication too is anticipated in Poinsot 1632: 312/3–6: "If the object of external sensation [prescissively considered] exists in something produced by sense itself as in an image or effect, then that object will not be some thing sensed immediately but rather something sensed in the image, which image itself rather will be that which is sensed"—"Quodsi existat in aliquo sui ut in imagine vel effectu, non immediate videbitur, sed ut contentum in imagine, ipsa vero imago est, quae videtur." (Ah, if only Hume had read Poinsot on this point which he thought no one had ever considered in other than the modern perspective making of ideas themselves—*species expressae*—the direct objects of knowledge in sensation! Certainly he could never have written as he did in 1748: Sect XII, Part I. Hume in this regard is discussed in Deely 2009b: Section 12.7–8., 152–156.)

Aristotle are not *semeia* in a less than generic sense at all, but must be regarded rather as σύμβολα (arguably a species of σημείον generically considered). The "words of language" belong thus to nature *and* to culture—but in entirely different and unconnected ways, considering only *direct* connections.

3.8.3.2. In the first case, we are regarding the words primarily in their physical being as sounds emitted by the animal, natural phenomena in the quite precise sense of forming part of the physical universe with its distinctive character of το όν, what the Latins will call *ens reale* or "mind-independent being" (because it need not be known in order to exist — in the present case, a physical vibration or mark on some surface is what it is, even when no one regards it).

3.8.3.3. But in the second case, we are regarding the words as cultural creations, instruments of conventions which differ between Greeks and barbarians, and barbarians among themselves.[49] They are not simple creatures of nature at all, but rather manifestations and expressions of *interpretations* (and hence of the *species expressae* discussed in Section 3.3., p. 56ff. above, in contrast to the *species impressae*, which last are what constitute most properly and directly *passiones animae* both at the sensory and perceptual levels, as also at the intellectual level of the *species intelligibiles* rendered by the activity of the intellect out of the phantasms as *species expressae* of the animal Umwelt).

3.8.3.4. Thus if we consider the words in our triangle as sounds or marks, they are related to the passions of the soul as "signs", all right,

---

[49] Poinsot discusses these differences quite pointedly in his 1632 *Tractatus de Signis* in Book III, Question 4 — e.g., 337/31–41: "we say that concepts signify the same thing for all when they are about the same object and have been formed in the same way; for they are natural similitudes. Thus all non-ultimate concepts representing expressions (or voices) inasmuch as they are significative represent the same thing for all those among whom they are so formed. But if they are not so formed among all hearing them, owing to the fact that not all know the signification of the voices, then the concepts of the voices were not concepts of the same thing, and so will not signify the same thing for all." So we can also say of the passions themselves at their most primary *sentire* level: even here there is more diversity among organisms within a species than was realized in the pre-evolutionary perspective of Aristotle and the Latins—so much so that it may even be said that, as Kalevi Kull remarked to me on the point, there is in some respects more uniformity at the level of words as governed by customs within culture than there is at the level of passions themselves as induced by the action of the sensible surroundings upon the sense organs of animals, working their way up through the *species impressae* first of internal sense and then of understanding.

but only in one of the specific Greek senses of *semeia*, in this case natu-ral signs such as practitioners of medicine rely upon—symptoms. As *semeia*, words are *symptoms* manifesting the presence in the speaker (or writer) of an underlying cognitive psychological state, the existence of which the words manifest, of which the words are "symptoms"—no different in this regard than groans manifesting pain. They are outward manifestations, whether Greek or barbarian, of an inward condition of the organism engaged in linguistic communication; and this without regard for what that communication may be or be intended to be.

3.8.3.5. But if we look back the other way, and consider the words not merely symptomatically but in terms of their *involvement with an intention or desire to communicate,* that is to say, as the result of a kind of choice made on the part of the speaker within a linguistic tradition ("*langue*")—if we consider the words not merely as sounds or marks symptomatic of a psychological state, but rather as instruments fash-ioned for the purpose of communicating some content of awareness — in this way the words appear not as *semeia* or symptoms primarily at all but rather as *symbola*. The huge difference between the two is pre-cisely the divide between *nature* and *culture* in the ancient way of understanding the two as oppositional.

3.8.3.6. Here we can understand Aristotle's realization that some "other science" than logic is required to understand the relation of words as words to the passions of the soul, and also his precipitousness in identifying that "other science" with psychology (*de anima*), for no realization existed as yet of culture as[50] "that minuscule segment of nature some anthropologists grandly compartmentalize as culture". Saussure in fact makes virtually the same mistake as Aristotle in this regard, even though he did indeed realize that the required "other sci-ence", for which he proposes the name "semiology", is one that did not exist in Aristotle's day. For Saussure saw, as Broden puts it (2009: 16), that "whereas psychology may study pure ideas and physics raw sounds", what is required to understand the words of language as *signs* —and hence the *signs* of language—is rather a science which "investi-gates a phenomenon in which the two [psychology and physics] interact and condition each other at every turn."[51]

---

[50] Sebeok 1984b: 2; cf. Deely 2010.

[51] Just this interaction is what is wanting in Poinsot's analysis of "ultimate and nonultimate" linguistics concepts, mentioned in note 40 above. It is precisely to mark and to foreground the interdependence of words and ideas, Broden points out (citing Saussure i.1907–1911: 103, 111–117), that "Saussure intro-duces [his] pair of neologisms: the sign comprises the signifier (cf. sound)

3.8.3.7. Linguistics does this, indeed;[52] and shows in so doing precisely how linguistic communication constitutes a secondary modeling system exapted from the primary adaptive modeling system of the human animal Innenwelt in its biologically underdetermined aspect, as we saw in Section 3.6.5. above. But the required science must do something more even than this: it must include within its purview the interaction within experience as a whole (inseparable from the zoösemiotic components of sensation and sense-perception) between ideas and things in the very process—semiosic to the core—of objectification as it begins even before the formation of those ideological other-representations which come to expression in language and open the path to yet a third modeling system, namely, the world of culture. For the realm of culture, as distinct from the social organization and interaction typical of all higher animals, is accessible directly only through language in the species-specific sense of anthroposemiosis as transformative of the Umwelt from a closed objective world biologically defined to an Umwelt open cosmologically.

3.8.3.8. The huge gap between nature and culture oppositionally

---

and the signified (cf. concept), such that the Janus linguistic entity resembles the sides of a single sheet of paper". Adding the interaction of bodies as also subsumed into language through the passions of the soul is required, then, to complete the triadic structure of the linguistic sign in the web of experience, larger than language, which ties the human animal into the biosphere shared with every life form, and not only into the semiosphere of culture within the biosphere. "Language is" indeed as Saussure insists (i.1907–1911: 122) "a form" constituted by relations "and not a substance": but no dyad or combination of dyads make up a sign properly speaking, but only a triadic relation wherein one thing stands for another to or for some third. Dyads as such always reveal Secondness, essential in the shaping of Thirdness from Firstness, indeed, but never itself the necessary *vis a prospecto* distinctive of semiosis.

[52] Saussure's post-1907 "strategic move is to say that while cumulatively and over time, 'analogy occupies a preponderant place in the theory of evolution' of languages, analogical creations as such illustrate not so much linguistic change but rather the synchronic functioning of language conceived as a virtual system and as en-ergeia, as a complex of 'generative forms'" (Broden 2009: 13). In this synchronic functioning, which is not a segment of any diachrony, but (Lotman 1990: 6) a homeostatic "bearer of the relationships which make up the essence of language" ("synchrony is homeostatic while diachrony is made up of a series of external and accidental infringements of it, in reacting against which synchrony re-establishes its integrity"), Saussure (i.1907–1911: 169) points out that "language never stops interpreting and decomposing the units given to it", so that it becomes over time (ibid. 172) "a garment covered with patches cut from its own cloth".

conceived is precisely the divide that Augustine will identify, subsume, and transcend semiotically with his seldom fully considered distinction[53] between *signa naturalia* and *signa data*. The later Latins will put the point more generally (but no longer including the signs of the plant world, as did Augustine's first general division of the *signa data*) by remarking that the action of signs transcends the divide between what stems from the order of *ens reale* first of all and what stems, rather, first of all and primarily, from the order of *ens rationis*, mind-dependent being, the order of culture and convention as shaping the world of nature to its own ends and purposes. Passions are related to words as their cause, insofar as the words are *semeia*; but, insofar as the words have an overlying relation *back* to passions as *symbola* thereof, the passions are related to the words as providing *directly* their communicative content (itself received *directly* from the surrounding "things" which thus 'inform' the words *indirectly* even though the *direct* 'application' of the words is *to the things* and not *to the developed passions* which—symbolically—provide the words with their 'content' directly and their iconicity indirectly, as Jakobson emphasized in underscoring the σύμβολα/σημείον entanglement on the words/passions side #3 of the triangle).

3.8.3.9. Here, then, is where account must be taken of what Lotman[54] described as "the 'debate' between those two linguists of genius, Saussure and Jakobson", over the sufficiency of the claim that "arbitrariness" is the identificative foundation of the linguistic sign. As we see now clearly, thanks to an examination of Aristotle's triangle within the perspective of the major tradition of semiotics after Sebeok, a symbolic relation—the relation alone which *of its very nature* contains an element of arbitrariness—is involved *both* in the relation of words to passions *and* in the relation of words to things. But, as we have taken care to see, *only* in the relation of words to things is the symbolic relation the *only* relation: *only* there, which is emphatically *not* where Saussure placed his *signifiant/signifié* relation, does arbitrariness "stand alone", as it were, in characterizing the linguistic sign with a symbolic dimension.

3.8.3.10. In the connection between words and thoughts, by contrast, which *is* where Saussure (counter-intuitively to the common use of language, as we noted in 3.8.1. above) placed his *signifiant/signifié* relation, there is *also* involved a relation of symptomaticity. From this involvement *inevitably natural language*[55] "*acquires secondary features of*

---

[53] On this point, see Deely 2009b: Section 6., 35–56.

[54] Lotman 1990: 17.

[55] In Lotman's 1990: 17–18 summary of Jakobson's argument against Saussure, italics added.

iconism" along with and de facto inseparable from whatever arbitrarity the symbolic relation in this case sustains, proving "Potebnya's [1862] idea that the entire sphere of language belongs to art". That is to say, natural language conveys, along with whatever "arbitrariness" attaches to the words as symbols, *also* secondary iconic features without which the element of arbitrariness ceases to belong to a *natural* language (as evidenced, for example, in the delusional thesis of "Analytic Philosophy" after Kripke that proper names in natural language are "rigid designators"—surely the prime illustration in late modern philosophy of what Sebeok frequently described as "looking in the destination for what should have been sought in the source" or, on one alternate occasion, as a "deluded misconstrual of the facts of the matter").

3.8.3.11. And remember, here, in the earliest decades of "philosophy", we are in the world of cenoscopic science only, and in its initial phase of development as "ancient philosophy among the Greeks": there is no general notion of sign as yet considered as common to nature and culture, such as we will find for the first time mainly in and after the work of Augustine.[56] Thus, the words of the triangle manifest a twofold relation that is not at all symmetrical: looked at from the side of the passions, the words are symptoms of a psychological state; but looked at from the side of the words, the passions are symbolically conveyed—not as to their existence but rather as to their content. The former standpoint reveals only, or at least primarily, a phenomenon of nature, the latter standpoint only, or at least primarily, a phenomenon of convention and culture.

3.9. "Alterius Est Enim Negotii":
Exactly What Is the Presupposed "Investigation Distinct" from Logic and Linguistic Interpretation Required for Correctly Understanding the Triangle?

Now let us consider this whole matter of the triangle no longer in the traditional perspective of Aristotle himself; nor for what it shows us of the insufficiency for semiotics of the Saussurean model of sign; nor

---

[56] See Deely 2009b for the most detailed treatment so far, but a treatment inspired above all by the work of Manetti 1987, which I first learned of through the work of Eco, Lambertini, Marmo, and Tabarroni 1984 and 1986, which Eco made me aware of in his opening lectures for our team-taught course on the "Historiographical Foundations of Semiotics" for the International Summer Institute for Semiotics and Structural Studies held in 1983 at Indiana University, Bloomington.

even in the perspective of the Aristotelian commentary tradition known as Scholasticism, which grew up with the institution of the universities as its basic skeletal structure until well into the 18th century. At that historical epoch—the 18th century—it became possible no longer to conceive of university education in exclusively cenoscopic terms, and place had to be yielded and made for the institutionalization of ideoscopy that we know as modern science, in contrast to cenoscopy (and in that sense also to semiotics, inasmuch as the doctrine of signs, as Peirce put it,[57] is a cenoscopic science underlying all other science—the point the Enlightenment missed).

Let us consider our seminal triangle, inherited from Aristotle, now simply in the light of Augustine's discovery that there is a general notion of sign that is common to the phenomena of nature and of culture, as also in the light of Poinsot's realization that relation is singularly indifferent to the division of nature from culture and mind-independent from mind-dependent being (in that one and the same relation can belong at different times to either order, depending upon nothing in the being of relation as suprasubjective but only upon the circumstances under which that suprasubjective being is realized here and now).

With the establishment between the Conimbricenses (1606/07) and Poinsot's own work (1632) that the being proper to signs consists precisely in a relation that is not only suprasubjective (as are all relations) but also triadic (as are all *sign* relations), the distinction that was drawn by Aristotle and the ancients between σημεῖον (as belonging exclusively to nature) and σύμβολον (as exclusively cultural)[58] breaks down. Indeed, the whole distinction between signs as external material objects and concepts (both generically animal and specifically human concepts, all *species expressae*, as Poinsot would point out)[59] as internal psychological states—i.e., in modern terms, the basic distinction between "inner" and "outer"—breaks down with the realization that any given particular, physical or psychological, functions as a "sign" (or rather, provides the vehicle for a signification) when and only when it occupies the foreground position of representing another than itself to or for some third within and under a triadic relation unifying all three terms in one signification.

In that case, the foundational investigation for the elements and terms of the triangle with which Aristotle opens his discussion of logical interpretation is no longer or primarily the *Treatise on the Soul*, where the notions of *sentire*, *phantasiari*, and *intelligere* are discussed in their

---

[57] Peirce 1908: CP 8.343, in a draft of a letter to Victoria Lady Welby.

[58] Useful to read in this connection is Eco 1986.

[59] Poinsot 1632: *Treatise on Signs*, Book II, Question 2, 240–253.

common terms and distinctive developments, but rather the *doctrina signorum*—the "doctrine of signs" spoken of in common by Poinsot, Locke, Peirce, and Sebeok[60]—as able to constitute a body of knowledge in its own right studying what all other bodies of knowledge and fields of investigation take for granted, namely, the action of signs.

Precisely here, as I intimated above, does Poinsot, in discussing *perihermenias*, go beyond Aristotle. The "distinct and prior investigation" to which the full understanding of the triangle belongs turns out to be not the ancient *De Anima* (neither psychology in the narrower modern sense nor general biology, as we might say today, for the expression "de anima" applied to the whole living world, plants and brute animals no less than human animals), but rather the doctrine of signs. Not at all coincidentally, this investigation into signs is exactly how and where Poinsot introduces his *Tractatus de Signis*, that earliest systematic treatment wherein the being of signs as triadic relations is first established and demonstrated:[61] "Because all the instruments of logical interpretation are constituted from signs, therefore, lest the foundations of the expositions of logic and propositions go unexamined, we are obliged to take on the project of explaining the nature and divisions of signs as a special treatment of its own."[62]

3.10. The Need for *Intrinsic* (Not *Ad Hoc*) Interdisciplinarity at the Curricular Core of University Studies

Perhaps the principal task of the postmodern university is to determine how its institutional structure need best be modified to accommodate

---

[60] See esp. the terminological entry "Doctrine" in Sebeok, Bouissac, Eco, Pelc, Posner, Rey, and Shukman, Editors 1986: 214, for details of this oldest general expression to name the development called semiotic today. See also Deely 1976, 1977, 1982, 1993, 2006b, and 2006c.

[61] See Poinsot 1632: "Super Libros Perihermenias. Remarks on Aristotle's Books on Interpretation, explaining the relation of the *Treatise on Signs* to the Aristotelian tradition, its philosophical justification, and its presuppositions within the *Ars Logica*", 38/1–39/18, together with the "Fifth Semiotic Marker" immediately following (p. 40) in the 1985 first independent edition of Poinsot's 1632 *Tractatus de Signis*.

[62] Paraphrasing Poinsot 1632: 38/11–19, and 39/5–7, "Super Libros Perihermenias": "Sed tamen, quia haec omnia tractantur in his libris per modum interpretationis et significationis, commune siquidem Logicae instrumentum est signum, quo omnia eius instrumenta constant, idcirco visum est in praesenti pro doctrina horum librorum ea tradere, quae ad explicandam naturam et divisiones signorum in Summulis insinuata, huc vero reservata sunt. Nec enim tironum captui quaestiones istae de signis proportionatae sunt. Nunc autem in hoc loco genuine introducuntur .... Ut autem clarius et uberius tractaretur, visum est seorsum de hoc edere tractatum."

the maturation of a semiotic consciousness within intellectual culture. This task today is comparable in depth and importance to the task the universities of the 18th century faced yesterday, in having to determine how to accommodate that maturation of ideoscopic consciousness we know today as modern science,[63] only now the problem is how to respond institutionally to Broden's accurate characterization[64] of "the last two centuries' trend toward increasing specialization and the fragmentation of knowledge".

Future thinkers, looking back a century hence on our situation today, are most likely to see the establishment of semiotics as a revolution, comparable in importance to the rebellion against scholasticism in the 17th century, except that the revolution in this case will have more the character of a *completion and maturation of scientific understanding* than an opposition to and rejection of the past. For just as the scientific revolution made specialization necessary, so the semiotic revolution will provide the antidote to specialization, not by rejecting ideoscopic specialization (as the authorities of the Scholastic Age in effect did) but through the realization of what all knowledge and experience have in common *including all specializations*, namely, a dependency upon semiosis as the action of signs, and hence the dependency of ideoscopy upon cenoscopy as something that needs to be molded into the institutional structure of the academy at the university level. As Daniel Taylor, one of my Spring 2008 university students, presciently put it: "Semiotics investigates what all the other disciplines seem to take for granted."

In this perspective, too, we can see that no small part of the reason why Aristotle's triangle proved as seminal as it has over philosophy's long history would be the fact that it augured the essential elements that had to be addressed in order to achieve an understanding of the being proper to signs as relational and irreducibly triadic. It is a triangle concerning "the meaning of meaning", all right, as Ogden and Richards brought to the fore (and in particular to Sebeok's attention in his undergraduate time in England); but the words/things/thoughts triangle is not correctly understandable as a "semantic triangle" *unless it is first and already understood* in semiotic terms as applicable to "meaning" throughout the order of animal Umwelts, even as it is for that very reason applicable within the Umwelt-as-Lebenswelt species-specific to semiotic animals.

---

[63] On this transition from cenoscopy to ideoscopy in the early modern period, see Deely 2008: esp. Chaps. 1 and 2. The failure of philosophy within the modern universities successfully to adapt to the dominance of idioscopy in modern intellectual life has best been attested to in the recent magnum opus of Ashley 2006, reviewed in Deely 2009c. Discussion also throughout Deely 2010a

[64] Broden 2009: 31.

In that sense, Aristotle's triangle, presemiotic in the perspective of his own time and writings (where the rational basis for the unity of speculative and practical thought had not yet successfully been determined),[65] was yet "virtually semiotic" in anticipation objectively of the work, first, of Augustine and Poinsot among the Latins, and then no less of Peirce in inaugurating semiotics as the postmodern turn of philosophy within intellectual culture as a whole.[66] And yet it turns out that a triangle cannot be the best way to symbolize the relation of *sign itself* as a triadic structure, for the very reason that Floyd Merrell has repeatedly pointed out: any triangle of its very nature lends itself to being regarded as a set of three binary relations, and hence to reinforcing linear, bivalent thinking (e.g., sign/signified, as if a dyad[67]), of the very sort that semiotics, in order to be achieved in its proper possibilities, had to move beyond.

So that ancient triangle of Aristotle, while it may not and, after all (as it turns out), *cannot* unqualifiedly symbolize the triadic sign, has nonetheless proved historically useful toward the development of semiotics. Let us conclude with a few words along that line of consideration—the usefulness of the triangle, despite its inappropriateness as a direct symbol of triadicity.

3.11. Triad in Contrast to Triangle

Perhaps the most remarkable and interesting thing about Poinsot's demonstration that the science presupposed to understanding logic and the inter-relations between words, thoughts, and things is not psychology ("*De anima*", whether ideoscopically or cenoscopically conceived), but rather the irreducibly cenoscopic science of semiotics as the doctrine of signs, is this development: that Aristotle's triangle, presented in his *De Interpretatione* as emblematic of psychology as the "science presupposed" to logic, quite disappears. For the sign, Poinsot has shown, considered in its proper being as sign, is neither an object nor a thing, but a relation irreducibly triadic, inasmuch as it is by *one*

---

[65] See Deely 2001: 261n28, and expansion of the point in Deely 2003: esp. the Section "Semiotica Utramque Comprehendit" in Chap. 6, 100–112.

[66] Deely 2011?; also 2009b, 2009c, 2001: Chaps. 15, 17, and 18; also Capozzi 1997.

[67] Within "ordinary language", that is exactly how "sign" tends to be conceived: we look up a term in a dictionary (sign as "word") and find there its meaning ("what the word signifies"). Completely hidden in the background to success in such a case is precisely the interpretant, which in this case is the habit-structure of one who knows the language in which the term is expressed and the dictionary is written, completing the triad essential to every actual achievement of "signification".

single relation, not two or any combination of twos, that the sign through its vehicle attains both *directly* its signified and *indirectly* its interpretant. All three—sign-vehicle, object-signified, interpretant—are thereby together unified under or through the one single triadic relation "constituting the mode of being of a sign", as Peirce put it,[68] and this triadic relation "is the proper and formal rationale of the sign", as Poinsot put it.[69] (Or, as Ketner, not glossing over the interpreter/interpretant distinction, summarized:[70] "A sign is the entire triadic relation whereby Something is represented by Something to Something".)

Thus, when Poinsot comes directly to treat of the very text, *De interpretatione* 16a3–8, which Aristotle opens with the presentation of his "words, things, passions" triangle,[71] Poinsot does not so much as mention a *triangle* image but passes directly to the *triadic* point[72] that "voces unica significatione significant res et conceptus", and "res principalius".[73] So it turns out that, when analyzed in semiotic terms, the sign is a triad but not a triangle properly speaking, even though the sign is commonly presented as such[74] simply because it involves three terms.

In fact, the question of how properly to represent the triadic sign relation, with or without recourse to triangles, is a puzzling one. I have

---

[68] Peirce 1904: CP 8.332.

[69] Poinsot 1632: *Tractatus de Signis* Book I, Question 3, 154/28–29.

[70] Ketner 1995: 32.

[71] Poinsot 1632: Appendix A "Whether vocal expressions primarily signify concepts or things", 344/1–351/40. The fuller treatment, i.e., the general point that signification consists in a triadic relation in all cases, not just the case of linguistic communication as species-specifically human, remains of course Poinsot 1632: Book I, Question 3, "Whether the relation of sign to signified is the same as the relation of sign to cognitive power".

[72] Ibid. 345/9–10.

[73] "nisi forte ipsa res significata sit conceptus vel eius intentio" — Ibid. 349/39–40.

[74] E.g., Blunden 2005/6: 4 of 14 (in PDF download from <http:// home. mira.net/~andy/works/semiosis.htm>), where he rightly states that "The basic schema of semiosis is the triadic relation", but then immediately diagrams it as a series of dyads in triangular formation, exactly as if to instantiate Merrell's repeated objection to the triangle representation of what is not triangular but triadic. Both involve three terms, yes; but both cannot be constituted from some combination of dyads; only the triangular (mis)representation allows for that. My own frequent use of triangular representations throughout *Basics of Semiotics* (Deely 1990 and after) is material, rather than formal, in that the irreducible triadicity of the sign is the formal point of the text as a whole repeated throughout its parts. The triangle as a representation remains materially convenient, if formally inadequate on its own terms.

so far been able to find only two, and both have their drawbacks.

The first representation is as what might be (and commonly has been, including by me) *misconstrued* as a "pre-triangle"—a figure that *would be* a triangle did it but have one more side—except for the (slight detail) that the "missing side" is *essentially* lacking (Figure 1). The problem, thus, is to represent *not* a triangle, but rather a *triad* which, like a triangle involves three "points" or "terms" but, unlike a triangle, does not have the three bilaterally connected, but connected rather by "one single relation which attains the second term directly and the third term indirectly" via the second.

Figure 1

The second representation is as what might be considered, for want of a better name, a tripod, but a tripod—"Merrell's Tripod", let me call it[75]—lacking a central connection as necessarily positive in the juncture of its "legs" (Figure 2). Thus:

Figure 2

It is as if we have to choose between a triangle with a missing side, and a tripod with a missing central connective. I will argue in a moment that this *"missingness"* is the strength of each of the diagrams. But first let me cite, in part at least (for one would have to gather many and lengthy passages from Merrell's writings to get a full grasp on hisun-

---

[75] As Floyd Merrell explained in the email accompanying the attachment of Figure 2 as reproduced here (essentially the same as the Figure 2 in his Sebeok Fellow Address 2006: 4): "I think tripod is necessary, since it is three-dimensional and the dimensions of time we live in are three-dimensional, which is no mere coincidence, given the categories, 3 in number. The 'psi', as well as +, -, square root of the central point, the empty set, and zero, would require pages to account for. ... As for the 'missing central connective', that's the reason for and the function of the square root at the central point of the tripod, about which the plus and the minus and the 'psi' symbols 'oscillate' (to create what you call a 'spiral'), and it is fed by the empty set and zero, or what Peirce called 'nothingness', or Buddhist 'emptiness'."

derstanding of this "tripod"), an explanation for Merrell's basic preference for some version of Figure 2:[76]

> The problem is [with any] Figure [that] ... still appears to be of
> bivalent orientation [such as we find in Saussure's *signifiant/signifié*
> model]. On the surface there is no more than a one-dimensional line
> severing a two-dimensional plane. In contrast, Figure 2, if construed
> as a tripod, offers a three-dimensional topological field.

> [I]t seems to me that with [this second figure], Firstness is poised
> to enter into signhood *as* something that is interdependently interre-
> lated *with* something else *for* someone or something *in* some respect or
> capacity. So the diagram is the bare beginning of a sign. It is a pre-
> sign, so to speak, the possibility of an actual concrete sign. I would
> suggest that the Firstness of this pre-sign, when emerging into mind-
> fulness, can take on its own Secondness, and then mediating
> Thirdness emerges. In other words ... Signhood. And the process con-
> tinues, without end.

On this accounting, Floyd's tripod amounts to a version of what I
have diagramed rather as the "semiotic spiral"[77] (of abductions, deduc-
tions, and retroductions[78] through which experience is constituted and
by which it develops, indeed, from conception to death), but one which
properly centers the process on "signhood" as a constantly emerging
form of being ever new.

But emerging whence, emerging from where? And this question
leads me to what I regard as the strength of both diagrams, namely, the
"missing" elements—be it the "triangle" with only two sides, or the
"tripod" with no connecting center: the explicit incorporation of *nonbeing* into the representation of sign.

A little noted, yet decisively important, feature of the action of
signs is that signs provide the only example of causality which functions equally in absence and in presence, the only instance of causality
between terms which need not all exist at the time of, and in order to

---

[76] Merrell 2006: 4, and 2004: 268–269. The situation of the sign as tripodically
diagramed, as Merrell says, is "more complicated, infinitely more complicated", than the bare diagram suggests; so let me share with the reader "a few
sources of the gyrating, spiraling, swirling and swiveling 'tripod':" Merrell
2000, 2007, 2007a, 2008, 2008a, 2008b.

[77] Deely 1985: 321, 2001: 28, 2003: 164, 2004a: 10, 2009b: 226.

[78] On the terminology here as I employ it, especially regarding this term "retro-
duction" used here in what amounts to a coinage, see Deely 2009b: 209 text
and note 9. In brief summary: abduction = getting an idea from experience of
things; deduction = seeing or drawing out the consequences of an idea; retro-
duction = returning to things to verify or disprove the consequences of a
developed idea.

complete, the sign action. Poinsot, one of the few so far to address directly the causality proper to the action of signs,[79] explains the element of nonbeing in semiosis as arising from the very nature of the triadic being proper to signs as relations: relations cannot be directly affected or changed except indirectly, by changing the objects or things related, whence the change in relations between them follows. So signs, insofar as consisting in relations, are powerless directly to affect outcomes except through their vehicles and significates acting under the relation of signification which makes them to be what they are, not in themselves, but in *the position they occupy* under the triadic relation of what Merrell felicitously terms "signhood".

This indirectness and dependency upon changes or actions in the order of Secondness also explains how and why signs as instantiating Thirdness typically exhibit an *influence of the future* within the present, altering the relevance of past events and presaging—but all only indirectly, and without strict necessity—"what is to come" out of what has been and is.[80] This singularity of semiosic causality, then, springs directly from the singularity of relation itself as suprasubjective, which makes semiosis possible in the first place. Actual semiosis as Thirdness may occur only "in the land of the living", but a semiosis virtual and exercised intermittently in raising the physical universe itself from a condition of lifelessness toward the possibility and finally the actuality of life, like the flaring of a match which does not hold its would-be flame, results from this same element of "nonbeing" embedded at the heart of semiosis as a distinctive causal process at work within, entangled with, the "efficient" productive forces of brute Secondness.

In the case of evolution, for example—not only biological evolution, but that prior and encompassing cosmic evolution which biological evolution presupposes in order for life to have become possible in the first place—Secondness provides and explains that element of chance and selection at work as a *vis a tergo* in the whole of evolution. But only Thirdness, whether intermittent and virtual ("degenerate") in inorganic nature, or actual and quasi-constant in the vegetative world, or actual and constant in the world of animals ("genuine" and complete, as it were), provides that *vis a prospecto* which we experience as "meaning" in whatever form, fictional or real, delusional or provisional.

Thus, no matter how you look at it, the discovery (or realization) of semiosis at the heart of meaning and the thematization of semiosis as

---

[79] Poinsot 1632: *Tractatus de Signis* Book I, Question 5, "Whether to signify, formally considered, is to cause something in the order of productive causality", 193/1–203/32, esp. 194/30–197/17. See also Deely 2009d: "The full vista of the action of signs", 233–275, esp. Section 4.3, 261–269.

[80] Cf. Williams 2009.

semiotics constitutes a revolution at the heart of intellectual culture, and presents a challenge for rethinking the institutionalization of academic life in our universities. This challenge is the equal and counterpoint to the challenge that ideoscopic science presented to the exclusively cenoscopic thinkers of the medieval universities, as I have pointed out above. Aristotle's triangle may have been inherently pre-semiotic, but viewed semiotically it at least shows us the elements that have to be synthesized in order to understand what signs are and how they act. For the three poles of the triangle at least, in contrast to the three "sides", have each an involvement with Thirdness. While not themselves a triad as such (i.e., as the separate poles of a triangle), yet each of these poles itself covertly contains the three triads from which anthroposemiosis constantly emerges: words, which as material signs presuppose triadic relations in the context of society and culture; thoughts, which as psychological states cannot exist without giving rise to triadic relations within Firstness; and things, which cannot be as known except as signifieds derived from objects which themselves as such (i.e., as apprehended) belong directly to Thirdness, beyond (and even within) sensation (*sentire* prescissively distinguished from *phantasiari* and *intelligere*) inseparable from brute Secondness.[81]

3.12. Aristotle's Triangle of Triads

Aristotle's is not a semiotic triangle, but pre-semiotic. In fact, it turns out that there is, strictly speaking, no such thing as a semiotic *triangle*, if we understand the difference between a *triad*—which has three terms under one single relation, indeed, but never as such three "sides" (three bivalent relations each reducible to dyadicity, whether one-sided[82] or reciprocal[83])—and a *triangle* as an irreducibly three-sided figure. Yet Aristotle's triangle, that ancient triangle proposed in the early light of philosophy's ancient dawn, in what it has accomplished in provoking thinking in the direction of an eventual semiotic consciousness over the long centuries of the semiotic animal's slow-by-slow development of an ever-fuller "self awareness", may well be taken now to symbolize

---

[81] On this last point, that "object signified" says redundantly what "signified" or "significate" says sufficiently, and that "object" is a disguised and, historically at least, normally misleading way to speak of signifieds, read *Purely Objective Reality* (Deely 2009c).

[82] As in the case of words to passions looked at one way as *symbola*, yet looked at another way as *semeia* (symptoms); or of words to things as *symbola*, respecting which reciprocally the things themselves directly "say nothing".

[83] As in the case of the things themselves, which "say nothing" to the words directly but speak loudly, indexically and iconically, in reciprocity with passions.

the work that lies ahead in the fields of academia for the semiotic community, inevitably pushing philosophy as the basic cenoscopic science toward assuming its proper place in the "core curriculum" as integrative of the intellectual culture of the postmodern university.

Semiotics, an intellectual phenomenon mainly of the 20th century as regards its actual formation as a community of inquirers, we are now coming to realize is no less than the dawning of a new era of intellectual culture, a global era marked (thanks to semiotics) by a noetic renewal beyond the *ne plus ultra* of the modern epistemology systematized by Kant. Semiotics launches postmodernity as a new epoch of philosophy itself understood finally as a cenoscopic, not an ideoscopic, science, one itself—like all the sciences—born out of the action of signs, the doctrine, or thematized investigation and understanding of which, we call today "semiotics".

Chapter 4

Parting Summation

That is how I project the diachronic development within the synchronic perspective in which the 20th century became the locus for the establishment of the foundations for the 21st century's continued development and expansion of the community of inquirers focused on the action of signs. The "foundation," we have seen, was a veritable web to the original weaving of which Sebeok was the central figure, and it may also be said that Jeff Bernard was a key figure in ensuring some institutionalized continuation of that weave (in the IASS, the International Association for Semiotic Studies, especially) among survivors of the "founding era", such as Umberto Eco (1932-), Paul Bouissac (1934-), Myrdene Anderson (1934-), Floyd Merrell (1937-), Augusto Ponzio (1942-), myself (1942-), Roland Posner (1942-), Jesper Hoffmeyer (1942-), Richard Lanigan (1943-), Winfried Nöth (1944-), Lucia Santaella (1944-), Nathan Houser (1944-), Marcel Danesi (1946-), Eero Tarasti (1948-), Vincent Colapietro (1950-), Peeter Torop (1950-), Thomas Broden (1951-), Søren Brier (1951-), Göran Sonneson (1951-) Kalevi Kull (1952-), Ivan Mladenov (1953-), Susan Petrilli (1954-), Claus Emmeche (1956-), Frederik Stjernfelt (1957-), Don Favareau (1957-), André De Tienne (1962-), Paul Cobley (1963-), Kumiko Tanaka-Ishii (1969-), Dario Martinelli (1974-), among others who yet remain on the current scene of "unfolding synchronicity"—the "land of the living"—within semiotics.

I project the semiotic development out to the year 2075 or so; but of course, those who will be able synchronically to judge of my projection, while it will include some now living but rather young, it will not include me or my contemporaries cited in the pages above, any more than Sebeok or Saussure has been able to comment on my "view as of 2010". For whatever the far boundary of my own synchrony within the larger diachrony of semiotics, it cannot be that distant. "Time will tell."

Appendix

Sebeok's Synthesis:
the Tartu–Bloomington–Copenhagen School

Juri Lotman (28 February 1922–1993 October 28), a suspect figure for the Russian authorities of the Soviet era, is the single most prominent figure of so-called "Soviet semiotics", and the principal theorist of the Saussure-oriented "Tartu-Moscow School" of semiotics, with its idea of linguistic communication as the "primary modeling system" through which alone access is provided to the world of culture as the "secondary modeling system".

In the purview of this school, biology has a background rather than a central role (see Ivanov 2008—still, that is a considerable improvement over Saussure's own views, and perhaps explains Sebeok's determined interest in meeting Lotman personally); so it must be said that the "Tartu-Moscow School" in its original formation and development belongs determinately to what Sebeok identified as the "minor tradition" of semiological analysis within semiotics as the complete doctrine of signs or "major tradition" (Deely 1986). (Kalevi Kull, in an email dated 12 June 2009, has pointed out to me an important detail concerning Lotman's position within semiology: "a change can be dated to 1982, when Lotman read Vernadsky's work on biosphere and as a result coined his term 'semiosphere'. In the same year he attended a conference on theoretical biology, which also gave him ideas to turn towards a more organicist approach. This in its way has enhanced the following biosemiotic developments in Tartu.") By "major tradition", of course, Sebeok meant an understanding of signs in terms of their proper being as triadic and operative not only throughout the cultural world but also throughout the natural world as prior to, independent of, and influenced by culture.

However, there was an earlier Tartu scholar, a "cryptosemiotician" (that is, a late modern thinker involved with but not thematically aware of the doctrine of signs, still a prisoner theoretically of the solipsist epistemology of modern philosophy) named Jakob von Uexküll (8 September 1864–1944 July 25), who, with his theoretical and experimental explication of the Umwelt/Innenwelt distinction, Sebeok realized, had correctly identified what is truly the *primary* modeling system for the animal kingdom as including human beings. This primary modeling system, the animal Innenwelt, required only a distinctive adaptation to provide the root from which and basis upon which linguistic communication as an *exaptation* could be established as the species-specifically human avenue to the development of culture as yet a third-level modeling system transforming the animal Umwelt confined to awareness of objects in relation to the animal into a Lebenswelt open to an exploration of objects not only in relation to ourselves as animals but also as being "things in themselves" sometimes mind-dependent, sometimes mind-independent, but typically (and certainly initially) a combination of both.

With this remarkable synthesis, Sebeok achieved nothing less than a theoretical revolution within the development of the doctrine of signs, one which has proved to be the main foundation for the development of semiotics in the 21st century. Sebeok's synthesis brings the minor tradition "Tartu-Moscow School" into the mainstream of semiotic development, but the old name fails completely to manifest the revolution.

In the first place, Jakob von Uexküll has no association at all with the original name, despite the fact that his Umwelttheorie was developed exactly while he was associated, as would later be Lotman, with the Tartu University. In the second place, the old name embodies a commitment to the Saussurean dyadic model of sign in exactly the sense that the Poinsot-Locke-Peirce tradition (the "major tradition", as Sebeok pointed out, because it is the only tradition squarely based on the model of sign recognizing the irreducibly triadic character of semiosis as following upon the relational being of signs as such) had shown to be incompatible with the full extent of semiosis.

Beginning with Sebeok's own introduction of the notion and term "zoösemiotics" in 1963, followed by Krampen's proposal of "phytosemiotics" in 1981, semiotics by the turn of the century had definitively established the inadequacy of an exclusively linguistic or cultural model, and laid the foundations for the fuller development of today's biosemiotics, centrally spearheaded by work of Jesper Hoffmeyer (1993, 2000, 2008, 2008a), among others.

Thus, when we assimilate the work of von Uexküll to the name "Tartu", and view the work of Lotman no longer in the exclusively semiological terms in which it was originally cast but as assimilated now rather to the mainstream Poinsot-Locke-Peirce development as distinctively *post*modern in the synthesis achieved by Sebeok, and particularly when we take into account the biosemiotic development with its center in the work of Danish semioticians, we should speak now of the **"Tartu-Bloomington-Copenhagen School"** as the major development within the major tradition whereby the action of signs becomes conscious of itself and of its role in the universe as a whole through the metasemiosis species-specific to human animals as *semiotic animals*.

These are the only animals which not only use signs but also recognize that the being of signs involves but does not reduce to anything sensible, consisting rather in the invisible spiral of interweaving triadic relations which turn things into objects and objects into signs in creating that path which "leads everywhere in nature" (Emmeche 1994: 126)—including where human beings have never set foot.

Historically Layered References

ANDERSON, Myrdene, John DEELY, Martin KRAMPEN, Joseph
   RANSDELL, Thomas A. SEBEOK, Thure VON UEXKÜLL
 1984. "A Semiotic Perspective on the Sciences: Steps toward a
   New Paradigm", *Semiotica* 52.1/2 (1984), 7–47.
   Originally published as Toronto Semiotic Circle
   Monograph (1984, Number 5); subsequently reprinted in
   Thomas A. Sebeok, *I Think I Am a Verb* (New York:
   Plenum, 1986), 17–44.
ARISTOTLE (384–322BC).
   Note: our citations here are from the 12-volume Oxford
   edition prepared under W. D. Ross Ed. 1928–1952 (q.v.);
   for the convenience of the reader, after the abbreviation
   RM, we also give the pages where applicable to the more
   readily available one-volume edition of *The Basic Works
   of Aristotle* (New York: Basic Books, 1941) prepared by
   Richard McKeon as editor, using the translations of the
   Oxford edition. Chronology for the works is based on
   Gauthier 1970, as follows:
 c.330BC. *On the Soul* (trans. J. A. Smith; RM 533–603 complete).
 c.330BC. *On Interpretation* (*De Interpretatione*; trans. Edghill 1926).
ASHLEY, Benedict (3 May 1915–).
 2006. *The Way toward Wisdom. An interdisciplinary and intercultur-
   al introduction to metaphysics* (South Bend, IN: University of
   Notre Dame Press).
BAER, Eugen.
 1986. "The Medical Symptom", Reading 13 in Deely, Williams,
   and Kruse 1986: 140–152; reprinted from *The American
   Journal of Semiotics* 1.3 (1982), 17–34.
BARBIERI, Marcello.
 2009. "Remarks in Response to [Champagne 2009] 'A Note on
   Barbieri's Scientific Biosemiotics'," *The American Journal of
   Semiotics* 25.1– 2 (2009), 163–166.
BARTHES, Roland (12 November 1915–1980 March 26).
 1964. *Éléments de sémiologie* (Paris: Éditions du Seuil).
BEKKER, August Immanuel (21 May 1785–1871 June 7), Editor.
 1831. *Corpus Aristotelicum* (Berlin: Prussian Academy of
   Sciences). The identification of a text by page and column
   from this edition has become the universal standard for
   citations of Aristotle.
BERGSON, Henri (18 October 1859–1941 January 4).
 1907. *L'Évolution créatrice* (Paris: Librairies Félix Alcan et

Guillaumin Réunies). Authorized English trans. by Arthur Mitchell, *Creative Evolution* (New York: Henry Holt & Company, 1911; reprinted New York: Modern Library, 1941).

BEUCHOT, Mauricio, and John DEELY.
    1995.   "Common Sources for the Semiotic of Charles Peirce and John Poinsot", *Review of Metaphysics* XLVIII.3 (March), 539–566.

BLUNDEN, Andy.
    2005/6. *The Subject. Philosophical Foundations. Charles Sanders Peirce: The Subject as Semiosis.* PDF download from <http://home.mira.net/~andy/works/semiosis.htm>.

BOETHIUS, Anicius Manlius Severinus (c.480–524AD).
    Migne (q.v.) has presented in his PL vols. 63 & 64 the main *versiones Boethii* extant to our time, though not in the form of critical editions. The main works useful to the present study appear in Vol. 64, *Manlii Severini Boetii opera omnia, non solum liberalium disciplinarum, sed etiam majorum facultatum studiosis utilissima, mo et sine quibus Aristoteles in praecipuis locis intelligi non potest,* etc. [Bibliothecae Cleri universae]. Dating of the works of Boethius is something of a scholarly nightmare. I have used for the works from PL 64 the dating worked out in Cappuyns 1937 (q.v.). Dating for nine of these works has been further examined in de Rijk 1964 (q.v.), and, for the convenience of other researchers, I have included the variant dates from de Rijk in square brackets after the dates of Cappuyns.

    c.AD511/13 [c.515/16]. *In librum Aristotelis de interpretatione libri sex. Editio secunda, seu Commentaria major;* PL 64 cols 394–638.

BOUISSAC, Paul.
    1979.   "A Compass for Semiotics" (review of Sebeok 1976), *Ars Semeiotica* 2.2, 205–221.

    1984.   "A Program for Semiotics": see under Gardin et al., below.

BRODEN, Thomas F.
    2009.   "Ferdinand de Saussure and Linguistic Structuralism", in Ingram ed. 2009: in press; page references are to prepublication pdf file.

CAJETAN, Thomas de Vio (20 February 1469–1534 August 9).
    1507.   *Commentaria in summam theologicam. Prima pars* (Rome: May 2). Reprinted in the Leonine edition of the *Sancti Thomae Aquinatis Doctoris Angelici Opera Omnia,* vols. 4 and 5 (Rome, 1888-1889), used in preparing the present work.

CAPOZZI, Rocco, Editor.
    1997.   *Reading Eco. An Anthology* (Bloomington: Indiana University Press, 1997).

CAPPUYNS, Maïeul (1901–).
   1937.   Entry "Boèce" in *Dictionnaire d'Histoire et de Géographie Ecclésiastiques*, tome neuvième (Paris: Librarie Letouzey), columns 347–380.
CAVARNOS, Constantine.
   1975.   *The Classical Theory of Relations. A study in the metaphysics of Plato, Aristotle, and Thomism* (Belmont, MA: Institute for Byzantine and Modern Greek Studies).
CHAMPAGNE, Marc.
   2009.   "A Note on M. Barbieri's 'Scientific Biosemiotics'," *The American Journal of Semiotics* 25.1– 2 (2009), 155–161.
CHANDLER, Daniel.
   2002.   *Semiotics: The Basics* (Milton Park, UK: Routledge).
               The title of this book is seriously misleading. *Semiology: Some Basics* would be immeasurably more appropriate, inasmuch as the book actually treats parts of semiotics focused exclusively on culture, and derives less from such primary sources of semiological tradition as Saussure, Barthes, or Greimas than it does from later sources in the area of media studies.
COBLEY, Paul.
   2009.   "Introduction", *The Routledge Companion to Semiotics*, ed. Paul Cobley (London: Routledge), 3–12.
   2009a. "Foreword" to Petrilli 2009: vii–x.
COBLEY, Paul, Editor.
   2009.   *The Routledge Companion to Semiotics* (London: Routledge).
   2009a. *Realism for the 21st Century. A John Deely Reader* (Scranton, PA: Scranton University Press).
COBLEY, Paul, John DEELY, Kalevi KULL, Susan PETRILLI, Editors.
   2009.   *Semiotics Continues to Astonish ... How Thomas A. Sebeok shaped the future of the doctrine of signs*, ed. Paul Cobley, John Deely, Kalevi Kull, and Susan Petrilli (Berlin: Mouton de Gruyter); a postmortem festschrift to the memory of Thomas Sebeok as the principal architect of semiotics in its postmodern development (Berlin: Mouton de Gruyter).
COLAPIETRO, Vincent Michael (2 November 1950–).
   1989.   *Peirce's Approach to the Self. A Semiotic Perspective on Human Subjectivity* (Albany, NY: State University of New York Press).
COLETTA, John.
   2008.   "Where 'Circular Patterns' of Self-Organizing Stones Meet Cell Walls and Fairy Circles: The Limits of Physiosemiosis", in Deely and Sbrocchi, eds. 2008: 197–202.

CONIMBRICENSES.
    1607.   *The Conimbricenses. Some Questions on Signs* (Milwaukee,
             WI: Marquette University Press, 2001), being the first time
             in English bilingual critical edition, prepared by John P.
             Doyle, from "De Signis", Chapter 1 of the Conimbricenses'
             commentary on Aristotle's *De Interpretatione*, in
             *Commentarii Collegii Conimbricensis et Societatis Jesu. In
             Universam Dialecticam Aristotelis Stagiritae. Secunda Pars*
             (Lyons: Sumptibus Horatii Cardon, 1607), pp. 4–67. An ear-
             lier edition minus the Greek text of Aristotle was published
             at Coimbra itself in 1606. This work is one of the milestones
             in the achievement of semiotic consciousness: see the dis-
             cussion in Beuchot and Deely 1995.
CROMBIE, I. M.
    1962.   *An Examination of Plato's Doctrine* (London: Routledge &
             Kegan Paul), 2 vols. Vol. 1, pp. 9–14, contains a discussion
             of the chronology of Plato's writings.
DE RIJK, Lambert Marie.
    1964.   "On the chronology of Boethius' works on logic I & II",
             Vivarium II.1 & 2 (May and November), pp. 1–49 and
             125–162, respectively.
DEELY, John N.
    1975.   "'Semeiotica': Dottrina dei segni". *Renovatio*, X, no. 4 (otto-
             bre-dicembre) pp. 472–490.
    1976.   "The Doctrine of Signs: Taking Form at Last", *Semiotica*
             18:2, 171–193. Essay review of Umberto Eco, *A Theory of
             Semiotics*, English trans. by David Osmond-Smith
             (Bloomington: Indiana University Press) of *Trattato di semi-
             otica generale* (Milan: Bompiani, 1975).
    1977.   "'Semiotic' as the Doctrine of Signs", *Ars Semeiotica* 1/3,
             41–68.
    1978.   "What's in a Name?", *Semiotica* 22.1–2, 151–181. Essay
             review of Thomas A. Sebeok, *Contributions to the Doctrine of
             Signs* (Bloomington, IN, and Lisse, Netherlands:
             Publication of the Research Center for Language and
             Semiotic Studies of Indiana University, together with The
             Peter De Ridder Press). Reprinted with an extended
             Prefatory Essay by Brooke Williams Deely, "Challenging
             Signs at the Crossroads", evaluating the book in light of
             major reviews (=Sources in Semiotics IV; Lanham, MD:
             University Press of America, 1985).
    1982.   *Introducing Semiotic: Its History and Doctrine* (Bloomington:
             Indiana University Press).
    1982a.   "On the Notion 'Doctrine of Signs'", Appendix I in Deely

1982: 127–130.

1985.   "Semiotic and the Liberal Arts", *The New Scholasticism* LIX.3 (Summer), 296–322. The "second epsilon" mentioned in this work is a blunder, for the "first epsilon" in the Greek "semeiotic" is not an epsilon but an eta, thus: Σημειωτική. Spiral on p. 321.

1986.   "A Context for Narrative Universals. Semiology as a *Pars Semeiotica*", *The American Journal of Semiotics* 4.3–4 (1986), 53–68.

1986a.   "Doctrine", terminological entry for the *Encyclopedic Dictionary of Semiotics*, ed. Thomas A. Sebeok et al. (Berlin: Mouton de Gruyter), Tome I, p. 214.

1988.   "Semiosis. The Subject Matter of Semiotic Inquiry", in *Semiotics 1988*, ed. Terry Prewitt, John Deely, and Karen Haworth (Lanham, MD: University Press of America, 1989), 133–142.

1989.   "The Grand Vision", presented on September 8 at the 5–10 September 1989 Charles Sanders Peirce Sesquicentennial International Congress at Harvard University; published in Vincent Colapietro and Thomas Olshewsky, eds., *Peirce's Doctrine of Signs* (Berlin: Mouton de Gruyter, 1996; one of the several volumes of the Proceedings of the Harvard Peirce Congress), 45–67.

1989a.   "A Global Enterprise", Preface to Thomas A. Sebeok, *The Sign & Its Masters* (= Sources in Semiotics VIII; corrected 2nd printing; Lanham, MD: Univresity Press of America), vii–xiv.

1990.   *Basics of Semiotics* (1st edition; Bloomington, IN: Indiana University Press).

1991.   "Semiotics and Biosemiotics: Are Sign-Science and Life-Science Coextensive?", in *Biosemiotics. The Semiotic Web 1991*, ed. Thomas A. Sebeok and Jean Umiker-Sebeok (Berlin: Mouton de Gruyter, 1992), 45–75. Since revised as Chapter 6 "How Do Signs Work?" in Deely 1994a: 151–182.

1992.   "Philosophy and Experience", *American Catholic Philosophical Quarterly* LXVI.4 (Winter 1992), 299–319.

1992a.   "From Glassy Essence to Bottomless Lake", in *Semiotics 1992*, ed. J. Deely (Lanham, MD: University Press of America), 151–158.

1993.   "Locke's Proposal for Semiotic and the Scholastic Doctrine of Species", presented at the 3rd Midwest Seminar in the History of Early Modern Philosophy held at the University of Chicago 9–10 November 1991; published in *The Modern Schoolman* LXX (March 1993), 165–188.

1993a. "How Does Semiosis Effect Renvoi?", the Thomas A. Sebeok Fellowship Inaugural Lecture delivered at the 18th Annual Meeting of the Semiotic Society of America, October 22, 1993, St. Louis, MO; published in *The American Journal of Semiotics* 11.1/2 (1994), 11–61.

1994.   *The Human Use of Signs; or Elements of Anthroposemiosis* (Lanham, MD: Rowman & Littlefield).

1994a. *New Beginnings. Early Modern Philosophy and Postmodern Thought* (Toronto, Canada: University of Toronto Press).

1995.   "A New Beginning for the Sciences", presented at the November 2–6, 1995, Symposium "Semiotics as a Bridge between the Humanities and the Sciences" organized at Victoria College of the University of Toronto by Prof. Marcel Danesi; selected papers published in *Semiotics as a Bridge between the Humanities and the Sciences*, ed. Paul Perron, Leonard G. Sbrocchi, Paul Colilli, and Marcel Danesi (Ottawa: Legas, 2000), 103–116.

1997.   "How Is the Universe Perfused with Signs?" in *Semiotics 1997*, ed. C. W. Spinks and J. N. Deely (New York: Peter Lang, 1998), 389–394.

1998.   "Physiosemiosis and Semiotics", in *Semiotics 1998*, ed. C. W. Spinks and J. N. Deely (New York: Peter Lang, 1999), 191–197.

1998a. *The Red Book*, an essay on the beginning of postmodern times, text presentated to The Metaphysical Club of the University of Helsinki, Finland, in Fall, November 2, 2000, and now published on their websiteat <http://www.helsinki.fi/science/commens/papers/redbook.pdf>.

1999.   "Postmodernism and the Perfusion of Signs", in *Semiosis•Evolution•Energy. Toward a reconceptualization of the sign*, ed. Edwina Taborsky (Aachen, Germany: Shaker Verlag), 7–13.

2000.   "Semiotics as a Postmodern Recovery of the Cultural Unconscious", *Sign Systems Studies* 28, 15–48; paper developed in connection with eight hours of lectures delivered at the University of Tartu, Estonia, 19–20 October 2000.

2000a. *The Green Book* <http://www.helsinki.fi/science/commens/papers/greenbook.pdf>.

2001.   *Four Ages of Understanding. The first postmodern survey of philosophy from ancient times to the turn of the 21ˢᵗ century* (Toronto, Canada: University of Toronto Press).

2001a. "Physiosemiosis in the Semiotic Spiral: A Play of Musement", *Sign Systems Studies* 29.1, 27–46; publication of morning presentation made February 16 at the

International Colloquium "The Semiotic Threshold from Nature to Culture" organized by Winfried Nöth at the University of Kassel, Wz II, February 16–17, 2001. Spiral on p. 28.

2001b. "Umwelt", *Semiotica* 134–1/4 (2001), 125–135; Special Issue on "Jakob von Uexküll: A paradigm for biology and semiotics" Guest-Edited by Kalevi Kull.

2003.   *The Impact on Philosophy of Semiotics. The Quasi-Error of the External World, with a Dialogue Between a 'Semiotist' and a 'Realist'*. South Bend: St. Augustine's Press.

2003a. "On the Word Semiotics, Formation and Origins", *Semiotica* 146.1/4 (2003), 1–49. Winner of 23rd Mouton D'Or Award for best essay in the field published in the calendar year. See further 2004a.

2004.   *Why Semiotics?* (Ottawa, Canada: Legas). An expanded monograph treatment of 2003a above.

2004a. "Dramatic Reading in Three Voices: 'A Sign Is *What?*',", *The American Journal of Semiotics* 20.1–4 (2004), 1–66; edited version enacted by Chris Tennison and Jim Berhhard on YouTube under "semiotic sign": <http://www.youtube.com/view_play_list?p=E9651802BCDC14BF>.

2004b. "From Semiotic Animal to Semioethical Animal and Back", in *Macht der Zeichen, Zeichen der Macht/ Signs of Power, Power of Signs* (Festschrift für Jeff Bernard; =Trans-Studien zur Veraenderung der Welt 3), ed. Gloria Withalm and Josef Wallmannsberger (Wien: Lit. Verlag), 120–136.

2005.   "The Semiotic Foundations of the Human Sciences from Augustine to Peirce", *Recherche Sémiotique/Semiotic Inquiry* 22.1–2–3 (2003), 3–29. Presented on Friday, 26 March, at the International Congress "Semiotics and the Humanities" jointly organized by Chinese Academy of Social Sciences and International Association for Semiotic Studies Beijing, China 25–29 March 2004.

2005a. "Thomas Albert Sebeok (1920–2001)", in *The Dictionary of Modern American Philosophers* (Bristol, UK: Thoemmes Press), Vol. 4, 2183–2188.

2006.   "Augustine, Saint, Theory of the Sign", in *Encyclopedia of Language and Linguistics, Second Edition*, Keith Brown Editor-in-Chief (London: Elsevier), Vol. 1, 574–577.

2006a. "Semiotics, History of", in *Encyclopedia of Language and Linguistics, Second Edition* (London: Elsevier, 2006), Vol. 11, 216–229.

2006b. "On 'Semiotics' as Naming the Doctrine of Signs", *Semiotica* 158.1/4 (2006), 1–33.

2006c. "The literal, the metaphorical, and the price of semiotics: an essay on philosophy of language and the doctrine of signs", *Semiotica* 161–1/4 (2006), 9–74.

2007. "The Primary Modeling System in Animals", in *La Filosofia del Linguaggio come arte dell'ascolto: sulla ricerca scientifica di Augusto Ponzio/Philosophy of Language as the art of listening: on Augusto Ponzio's scientific research*, ed. Susan Petrilli (Bari, Italy: Edizione dal Sud), 161–179. Online at <http://www.augustoponzio.com/Critical/12._Deely.pdf>.

2007a. "Evolution, semiosis, and ethics: rethinking the context of natural law", in *Contemporary Perspectives on Natural Law*, ed. Ana Marta González (Aldershot, England: Ashgate, 2007), volume in preparation.

2007b. *Intentionality and Semiotics. A story of mutual fecundation* (Scranton, PA: University of Scranton Press).

2008. *Descartes & Poinsot: the crossroad of signs and ideas* (Scranton, PA: University of Scranton Press).

2008a. "How To Go Nowhere with Language", essay review of John O'Callaghan, *Thomist Realism and the Linguistic Turn* (Notre Dame: University of Notre Dame Press, 2003), *American Catholic Philosophical Review* 82.2 (Spring 2008), 337–359.

2009. "'To Find Our Way In These Dark Woods' *versus* Coming Up Short", a review-essay of Thomas Lloyd Short, *Peirce's Theory of Signs* (Cambridge: Cambridge University Press, 2007), in *Recherche Semiotique/Semiotic Inquiry* (RS·SI), 26.2–3 (2006), 57–126.

   Note on date discrepancy: This review essay was commissioned 11 April 2007, submitted in final form October 2007; actual publication was in January 2009. The issue 26 (2006) is a catch-up back issue, therefore, a phenomenon all too common with journals.

2009a. "A Short Farewell", a brief rebuttal of Short's "Response to John Deely" cited in the immediately preceding 2009 entry, published in *Recherche Semiotique/Semiotic Inquiry* (RS·SI), 27.1–2 (2007), in press (and, as was the case with the 2009 entry case, the actual publication was also to be in 2009).

2009b. *Augustine & Poinsot: the Protosemiotic Development* (Scranton, PA: University of Scranton Press).

2009c. *Purely Objective Reality* (Berlin, Germany: Mouton de Gruyter).

2009d. Fifth expanded edition, *Basics of Semiotics* (= Tartu Semiotics Library 4.2; Tartu, Estonia: Tartu University Press).

2009e. "Aristotle's Triangle and the Triadic Sign", Prologue to *Semiotics 2008*, ed. John Deely and Leonard Sbrocchi (Proceedings of the 33rd Annual SSA Meeting held in Houston, Texas, October 16–19, 2008; Ottawa, Canada: Legas), li–xc.

2009f. "In The Twilight Neothomism, a Call for a New Beginning. A return in philosophy to the idea of progress by deepening insight rather than by substitution", *American Catholic Philosophical Quarterly* 83.2 (Spring 2009).

2009g. "Postmodernity and the Unmasking of Objectivity", plenary lecture presented 7 June 2009 to the International Semiotics Institute (ISI) 2009 June 5–9 Summer School for Semiotic Studies in Imatra, Finland.

2009h. "The Unmasking of Objectivity", essay prepared at the requested of Professor Robert E. Wood as co-editor with Michael Baur of a Festschrift in Honor of Kenneth L. Schmitz, projected for 2009 publication by the Catholic University of America Press.

2009i. "The Full Vista of the Action of Signs", *Chinese Semiotic Studies* 1 (June 2009), 171–222.

2010. *Semiotic Animal. A postmodern definition of human being transcending Patriarchy and Feminism* (South Bend, IN: St Augustine Press).

2010a. *Medieval Philosophy Redefined* (Scranton, PA: University of Scranton Press).

2011? *Peirce & Poinsot. The action of signs from nature to ethics*, Volume 3 of the "Postmodernity in Philosophy" Poinsot trilogy (The University of Scranton Press was shut down by the University President in the Fall of 2010, with all existing contracts for books not yet in typesetting cancelled; so where this third volume in the Poinsot Trilogy will be published has yet to be determined).

DEELY, John N., and Leonard G. SBROCCHI, Editors.

2008. *Semiotics 2008* (Proceedings of the 33rd Annual Meeting of the Semiotics Society of America, held 16–19 October 2009 in Houston, Texas; Ottawa, Canada: Legas Publishing).

DEELY, John N., Brooke WILLIAMS, and Felicia E. KRUSE, Editors.

1986. *Frontiers in Semiotics* (Bloomington: Indiana University Press). Preface on "Pars Pro Toto", pp. viii–xvii; "Description of Contributions", pp. xviii–xxii. See also Deely 1986, above.

DESCARTES, René (31 March 1596–1650 February 11).

1649. *Les Passions de l'Ame* (1st ed.; Paris: Henry Le Gras); trans. by Stephen H. Voss as *The Passions of the Soul* (Indianapolis,

IN: Hackett Publishing Co., 1988).

DOYLE, John P. (1930–).

1984.   "The Conimbricenses on the Relations Involved in Signs", in *Semiotics 1984*, ed. John Deely (Proceedings of the Ninth Annual Meeting of the Semiotic Society of America; Lanham, MD: University Press of America, 1985), 567–576.

1998.   "The Conimbricenses on the Semiotic Character of Mirror Images", *The Modern Schoolman* LXXVI (November), 17–31.

DOYLE, John P., Editor and Translator.

2001.   *The Conimbricenses. Some Questions on Signs* (Milwaukee, WI: Marquette University Press), bilingual critical edition of Conimbricenses 1607, q.v.

ECO, Umberto (5 January 1932–).

1976.   *A Theory of Semiotics*, English trans. by David Osmond-Smith (Bloomington: Indiana University Press) of *Trattato di semiotica generale* (Milan, Italy: Bompiani, 1975). Reviewed in Deely 1976.

1986.   "On Symbols", the third appearance, with revisions, of a text first published in 1982, then in 1984, and finally as Reading 14 in Deely, Williams, and Kruse 1986: 153–180; see the editorial note on p. xx for the full provenance of this text.

1990.   *The Limits of Interpretation* (Bloomington: Indiana University Press).

ECO, Umberto, and John DEELY.

1983.   May 30–June 24. "Historiographical Foundations of Semiotics", course taught at ISISSS '83 (Indiana University, Bloomington campus). Complete cassette tapes of lectures exist but have never been transcribed.

ECO, Umberto, Roberto LAMBERTINI, Costantino MARMO, and Andrea TABARRONI.

1984.   "On Animal Language in the Medieval Classification of Signs", *Versus* 38/39 (maggio–dicembre), 3–38.

1986.   "Latratus Canis or: The Dog's Barking", Reading 6 in Deely, Williams, and Kruse 1986: 63–73; see the editorial note on the provenance of this text, ibid. p. xix.

EDGHILL, Ella Mary (13 November 1881– ?), Translator.

1926.   *[Aristotle] On Interpretation* (Whitefish, MT: Kessinger Publishing, 2004).

EMMECHE, Claus (1956–)

1994.   *The Garden in the Machine* (Princeton, NJ: Princeton University Press).

ESCHBACH, Achim, and Jürgen TRABANT, eds.

1983.   *History of Semiotics* (= Foundations of Semiotics, Vol. 7)

(Amsterdam: John Benjamins).

GARDIN, Jean-Claude, Paul BOUISSAC, and Kenneth E. FOOTE.
    1984.   "A Program for Semiotics", circulated for signatures June 15, 1984, at the Toronto ISISSS 84, subsequently published under the same title as a "Guest Editorial" in Semiotica 52–1/2, 1–5, and also presented by Paul Bouissac on October 10 to the "State-of-the-Art" Research Conference held at Indiana University, Bloomington, October 8–10.

GAUTHIER, René Antoine.
    1970.   "Introduction", being Tome I, vol. 1 ("Première Partie"), of *L'Éthique à Nicomaque*, traduction et commentaire par René Antoine Gauthier et Jean Yves Jolif (2nd ed. avec une Introduction nouvelle par Gauthier; Paris: Béatrice-Nauwelaerts), 2 tomes in 4 volumes (Introduction, Traduction, Commentaire livres I–V, Commentaire livres VI–X).

GODEL, Robert (1902–1984).
    1967.   *Les Sources manuscrites du* Cours de linguistique générale *de F. de Saussure* (Geneva: Droz).

GOMPERZ, Heinrich (18 January 1873–1942 December 27).
    1908.   *Weltanschauungslehre: ein Versuch die Hauptprobleme der allgemeinen theoretischen Philosophie geschichtlich zu entwickeln und sachlich zu bearbeiten* (Jena, Germany: E. Diederichs).

GOTTLIEB, Anthony.
    2001.   *The Dream of Reason. A History of Philosophy from the Greeks to the Renaissance* (New York, NY: W. W. Norton & Company).

GOULD, Stephen J., and Elisabeth S. VRBA.
    1982.   "Exaptation — A Missing Term in the Science of Form", Paleobiology 8.1 (Winter), 4-15.

GREDT, Josephus (13 July 1863–1940 January 20).
    1924.   *De Cognitione Sensuum Externorum. Inquisitio psychologico-criteriologica circa realismum criticum et objectivitatem qualitatum sensibilium* (ed. altera aucta et emendata; Rome: Desclée & Socii, Editores Pontificii).

GREIMAS, Algirdas Julien (9 March 1917–1992 February 27).
    1966.   *Semantique structurale, recherche de méthode* (Paris: Larousse).

GREIMAS, Algirdas Julien, and Joseph COURTÉS.
    1982.   *Semiotics and Language: An Analytical Dictionary*, trans. Larry Crist and Daniel Patte (Bloomington, IN: Indiana University Press).

HARDWICK, Charles S., Editor, with the assistance of James Cook.
    1977.   *Semiotics and Significs. The Correspondence between Charles S.*

· *Peirce and Victoria Lady Welby* (Bloomington: Indiana University Press).

HJELMSLEV, Louis (1899–1965)·

1961.   *Prolegomena to a Theory of Language,* being the second, revised translation by Francis J. Whitfield of *Omkring sprogteoriens grundlaeggelse* (Copenhagen: Ejnar Munksgaard, 1943), incorporating "several minor corrections and changes that have suggested themselves in the course of discussions between the author and the translator" (Hjelmslev and Whitfield 1961, page v of this volume).

HOFFMEYER, Jesper (21 February 1942–).

1993.   *En Snegl På Vejen: Betydningens naturhistorie* (Copenhagen: Rosinante), trans. by Barbara J. Haverland as *Signs of Meaning in the Universe* (Bloomington, IN: Indiana University Press, 1996).

1996.   *Signs of Meaning in the Universe Nature. The Natural History of Signification* (Bloomington, IN: Indiana University Press).

2000.   "The Central Dogma: A Joke that Became Real", the 3rd Sebeok Fellow address, delivered 29 September 2000 at the SSA Annual Meeting held at Purdue University; published in *Semiotica* 138–1/4 (2002): 1–13.

2002.   "The Central Dogma: A Joke that became Real" (29 September October 2000 address as fourth Sebeok Fellow), *Semiotica.* 138.1, 1–13.

2002a.   "Code Duality Revisited", http://www.library.utoronto.ca/see/SEED/Vol2-1/Hoffmeyer/Hoffmeyer.htm.

2008.   *Biosemiotics. An Examination into the Signs of Life and the Life of Signs* (= Approaches to Postmodernity, vol. 2; Sccranton, PA: University of Scranton Press), trans. from the Danish *Biosemiotik. En afhandling om livets tegn og tegnenes liv* (Charlottenlund, Denmark: Forlaget Ries, 2005) by Jesper Hoffmeyer and Donald Favareau, ed. Donald Favareau.

2008a.   "Biology is immature biosemiotics", Epilogue to the *Semiotics 2008* Semiotic Society of America Proceedings volume, ed. John Deely and Leonard Sbrocchi (Ottawa, Canada: Legas, 2009).

HOUSER, Nathan.

2006.   "Pragmaschism?", in *Semiotics 2006,* ed. Benjamin Smith and Terry J. Prewitt (Ottawa: Legas, 2009), 3–12.

INGRAM, David, Editor.

2009.   *Politics and the Human Sciences (1940–1968),* vol. 5 of the *History of Continental Philosophy,* Alan D. Schrift, General Editor (Stocksfield, England: Acumen).

IVANOV, Vyacheslav V.
    2008.   "Semiotics of the 20th Century", *Sign System Studies* 36.1, 185–244.

JAKOBSON, Roman Osipovich (11 October 1896–1982 July 18).
    1942.   "La théorie saussurienne en rétrospection", text ed. Linda Waugh, *Linguistics* 22.2 (1984): 161–196.
    1965.   "Quest for the Essence of Language", *Diogenes* 13.51, 21–37.
    1974.   "Coup d'oeil sur le développement de la sémiotique", in *Panorama sémiotique/A Semiotic Landscape*, Proceedings of the First Congress of the International Association for Semiotic Studies, Milan, June 1974, ed. Seymour Chatman, Umberto Eco, and Jean-Marie Klinkenberg (The Hague: Mouton, 1979), 3-18. Also published separately under the same title by the Research Center for Language and Semiotic Studies as a small monograph (= Studies in Semiotics 3; Bloomington: Indiana University Publications, 1975); and in an English trans. by Patricia Baudoin titled "A Glance at the Development of Semiotics", in *The Framework of Language* (Ann Arbor, MI: Michigan Studies in the Humanities, Horace R. Rackham School of Graduate Studies, 1980), 1–30.

KERECUK, Nadia.
    2006.   "Potebnja, Aleksander (1835–91)", in *Encyclopedia of Language and Linguistics*, ed. Keith Brown (2nd Ed. Elsevier: Oxford), Vol. 9, pp. 798–800.

KETNER, Kenneth L.
    1995.   "Novel Science: or How contemporary social science is not well and why literature and semeiotic provide a cure", in Samway Ed. 1995.

KRAMPEN, Martin (1928–).
    1981.   "Phytosemiotics", *Semiotica*, 36.3/4: 187-209. Reprinted in Deely, Williams, and Kruse, eds. 1986: 83–95.

KRETZMANN, Norman J. (4 November 1928–1998 August 1).
    1967.   "Semantics, History of", in *The Encyclopedia of Philosophy*, ed. Paul Edwards (New York: Macmillan Publishing Co., 1967), vol. 7, 367.1
    1974.   "Aristotle on Spoken Sound Significant by Convention", in *Ancient Logic and Its Modern Interpretations*, ed. John Corcoran (Dordrecht, Holland: D. Reidel Publishing Company, 1974), 3–21.

KULL, Kalevi.
    2005.   "Semiotics is a theory of life" (10 October 2003 address as fifth Sebeok Fellow), in *Semiotics 2003*, ed. Rodney

Williamson, Leonard Sbrocchi, and John Deely, eds. (Ottawa, Canada: Legas), 15–31.

LOTMAN, Juri (28 February 1922–1993 October 28).

1974. "Primary and Secondary Communication-Modeling Systems", in Lucid 1977: 95–98, being the translation of "O sootnošenii pervičnogo i vtroičnogo v kommunikativno-modelirujuščix sistemax" in *Materialy vsesojuznogo simpoziuma po vtoričnym modelirujuščim sistemam* 1.5 (Tartu: Tartu University Press), 224–228.

1987. "On the contemporary concept of text", in *Livstegn: Tidsskrift for Norsk forening for semiotikk* (Proceedings of the first symposium "Semiotics in Theory and Practice", 2–3 Oct. 1986, Bergen, Norway: Norwegian Association for Semiotic Studies) 3, 159–163 (trans. from Russian by Jostein Bortnes).

1990. *Universe of the Mind: A Semiotic Theory of Culture* (London: I. B. Taurus).

LOVELOCK, James Ephraim (26 July 1919–).

1979. *GAIA — A New Look at Life on Earth* (Oxford, England: Oxford University Press).

LUCID, David, Editor and Translator.

1977. *Soviet Semiotics. An Anthology* (Baltimore, MD: The Johns Hopkins University Press).

MANETTI, Giovanni (1 June 1949–).

1987. *Le teorie del segno nell'antichità classica* (Milan: Bompiani), trans. by Christine Richardson as *Theories of the Sign in Classical Antiquity* (Bloomington, IN: Indiana University Press, 1993).

MARITAIN, Jacques (18 November 1882–1973 April 28).

1959. *Distinguish to Unite, or The Degrees of Knowledge*, trans. from the 4th French ed. of *Distinguer pour Unir: Ou, les Degrés du Savoir* (Paris: Desclée de Brouwer, 1932) under the supervision of Gerald B. Phelan (New York: Scribner's).

MEIER-OESER, Stephan (3 October 1957–).

1995. Entry "Semiotik, Semiologie" in the *Historisches Wörterbuch der Philosophie*, ed. Joachim Ritter and Karlfried Gründer (Basel: Schwabe), Band IX, cols. 601–608.

1997. *Die Spur des Zeichens. Das Zeichen und seine Funktion in der Philosohie des Mittelalters und der frühen Neuzeit* (Berlin: Walter de Gruyter).

MERRELL, Floyd.

2000. *Signs for Everybody: Or, Communication, Quandaries, and Chaos* (Ottawa: Legas Press).

2004. "Signs so constructed that they can know themselves", *The*

American Journal of Semiotics 22.1–4, 3–26.

2006.   "Chewing Gum, Ambulating, and Signing, all at the Same Time: Or, The Magical Number Three" (6th Sebeok Fellow Address), *The American Journal of Semiotics* 22.1–4, 3–26.

2007.   *Processing Cultural Meaning* (Ottawa: Legas Press).

2007a.   "Toward a Concept of Pluralistic, Inter-relational Semiosis". *Sign Systems Studies* 35.1/2, 9–70.

2008.   "Is the Semiosic Sphere's Center Everywhere and its Circumference Nowhere?", *Semiotica* 169.1/4, 269–300.

2008a.   "Life before Matter, Possible Signification before Tangible Signs: Toward a Mediating View", *Cosmos and History* 4.1, 99–112.

2008b.   "Lotman's Semiosphere, Peirce's Signs, and Cultural Processes", *Russian Journal of Communication* 1.4, 372–400.

MIGNE, J. P. (1800–1875), Editor.

c.1844-1864. *Patrologiae Cursus Completus, Series Latina* (PL, customarily), (Paris), 221 volumes.

MORRIS, Charles.

1971.   *Writings on the General Theory of Signs* (= vol. 16 in "Approaches to Semiotics" series ed. by Thomas Sebeok; The Hague: Mouton).

NAVILLE, Adrien (1845–1930).

1901.   *Nouvelle classification des sciences* (2nd ed.; Paris: Alcan).

NEWSOME, Jonathan.

2008.   "Chemiosemiotics", in Deely and Sbrocchi, eds. 2008: 203–207.

O'CALLAGHAN, John.

2003.   *Thomist Realism and the Linguistic Turn* (Notre Dame: University of Notre Dame Press).

OGDEN, Charles Kay (1 June 1889–1957 March 21), and Ivor Armstrong RICHARDS (26 February 1893–1979 September 7).

1923.   *The Meaning of Meaning. A Study of the Influence of Language upon Thought and of the Science of Symbolism* (New York: Harcourt, Brace).

PEIRCE, Charles Sanders (10 September 1839–1914 April 19).

i.1866–1913. *The Collected Papers of Charles Sanders Peirce*, Vols. I–VI ed. Charles Hartshorne and Paul Weiss (Cambridge, MA: Harvard University Press, 1931–1935), Vols. VII–VIII ed. Arthur W. Burks (same publisher, 1958); all eight vols. in electronic form ed. John Deely with an Introduction "Membra Ficte Disjecta—A Disordered Array of Severed Parts" (Charlottesville, VA: Intelex Corporation, 1994). Dating within the CP is based on the Burks Bibliography at the end of CP 8. The abbreviation followed

by volume and paragraph numbers with a period between
follows the standard CP reference form.

1867–1893. *The Essential Peirce (1867–1893), Volume 1*, ed. Nathan
Houser and Christian Kloesel (Bloomington, IN: Indiana
University Press, 1992). The materials in this volume are
also found in the *Collected Papers*.

1893–1913. *The Essential Peirce (1893–1913), Volume 2*, ed. Nathan
Houser, André De Tienne, Jonathan R. Eller, Cathy L.
Clark, Albert C. Lewis, D. Bront Davis (Bloomington, IN:
Indiana University Press, 1998). The materials in this vol-
ume are from previously unpublished manuscripts.

1901.   "The Idea of a Law of Nature among the contemporaries of
David Hume and among advanced thinkers of the present
day"; CP 1.133–134 are from it.

1908.   Draft of a letter dated December 24, 25, 28 "On the
Classification of Signs", CP 8.342–379 except 368n23 are
from it (Burks p. 321 par. 20.b). In Hardwick ed. 1977:
73–86; and EP 2.478–483.

PETRILLI, Susan.

1988.   "Semioethics and Responsibility", *The American Journal of
Semiotics* 24.4 (2008), 3–48.

2004.   "Responsibility of Power and the Power of Responsibility:
From the 'Semiotic' to the 'Semioethic' Animal", in *Macht
der Zeichen, Zeichen der Macht/ Signs of Power, Power of Signs*
(Festschrift für Jeff Bernard; = Trans-Studien zur
Veraenderung der Welt 3), ed. Gloria Witthalm and Josef
Wallmannsberger (Wien: Lit. Verlag), 103–119.

2007.   "Abduction, Medical Semeiotics and Semioethics.
Individual and Social Symptomatology from a Semiotic
Perspective", *Model-Based Reasoning in Science, Technology,
and Medicine*, ed. Lorenzo Magnani and Ping Li (= Studies
in Computational Intelligence, Vol. 64, based on papers
presented at the international conference "Model-Based
Reasoning in Science and Medicine", held at Sun Yat-sen
University, Guangzhou, P.R. China, 3–5 July 2006; Berlin:
Springer), 117–130.

2008.   "Sebeok Fellow Plenary Address: Semioethics and
Responsibility. Beyond Specialisms, Universalisms, and
Humanisms", Essay #1 in the Sebeok Fellow Special Issue
of *The American Journal of Semiotics* 24.4, 3–48; now reprinted pagination unchanged in Petrilli 2010.

2009.   *Signifying and Understanding. Reading the Works of Victoria
Welby and the Signific Movement* (Berlin: Mouton de
Gruyter).

2010.   *Sign Crossroads in Global Perspective*, monograph hardcover reprint of the Sebeok Fellow Special Issue of *The American Journal of Semiotics* 24.4 (2008), with the addition of a new "Editor's Preface: In her own voice", vii–ix, and comprehensive Index, 303–330.

PLATO (c.427–c.347BC).

i.399–347BC. *The Dialogues of Plato*, which I have consulted in the trans. of B. Jowett (4th ed., rev.; Oxford,1953) and in the ed. of Edith Hamilton and Huntington Cairns, including the Letters (Pantheon Books: Bollingen Series LXXI, 1961). References to translators of Plato other than Jowett will be found in this Hamilton & Cairns collection. The dialogues are chronologized as follows, on the general basis of Crombie 1962: I, 9–14:

c.399–390BC, early dialogues presenting the life and teaching of Socrates: *Apology, Charmides, Cratylus, Crito, Euthydemus, Euthyphro, Gorgias, Hippias I ("Minor") and II ("Major"), Ion, Laches, Lysis, Menexenus, Meno, Protagoras;*

c.391–360BC, middle dialogues presenting Plato's own thought through the vehicle of Socrates: *Parmenides, Phaedo, Phaedrus, Republic, Symposium, Theatetus;*

c.359–347BC, late dialogues, treating sophisticated and 'semi-professional' issues: *Laws, Philebus, Sophist, Statesman, Timaeus, Critias.*

POINSOT, John (9 July 1589–1644 June 17).

1631–1635. *Cursus Philosophicus* (Alcalá, Spain, vols. 1 & 2, 1631 & 1632; Madrid, Spain, vol. 3, 1633; Alcalá, Spain, vols. 4 & 5, 1634 & 1635). The critical edition of Reiser 1948 "II Reimpressio emendata" vols. 1 & 2, vol. 3 1950, with *Thomisticus* added to the title of the whole, and in Vol. I "Introductory Remarks" by John Deely, pp. v–xiv, followed by an "Einleitende Bemerkungen" by Martin Walter, pp. xv–xl, and an Appendix "Bibliographie zu Johannes Poinsot" of 27 pages at the end of Vol. 3, was published by Hildesheim: Georg Olms Verlag, 2008.

1632.   *Tractatus de Signis*, trans. and ed. by John Deely in consultation with Ralph Austin Powell (Berkeley: University of California Press, 1985). Available in electronic form (Charlottesville, Virginia: Intelex Corporation, 1992). A corrected 2 ed. of this work, with new editorial materials, nd was published by St Augustine's Press (South Bend, IN) in the Fall of 2010.

PONZIO, Augusto, and Susan PETRILLI.

2003.   *Semioetica* (Roma: Meltemi).

2005.   *Semiotics Unbounded: Interpretive Routes through the Open Network of Signs* (Toronto, Canada: University of Toronto Press).
POTEBNIA, Aleksander (Oleksander O. Potebnia;1835–1891).
1862.   *Myslí' i jazyk* (Kharkov': Mirnyj trud.); an annotated English and Portuguese translation by Nadia Kerecuk has been announced several years ago, but I have not been able to find it actually published. See, however, Kerecuk 2006.
RUSSELL, Bertrand (18 May 1872–1970 February 2).
1945.   *A History of Western Philosophy* (New York: Simon & Schuster).
SAMWAY, Patrick H., Editor.
1995.   *A Thief of Peirce. The Letters of Kenneth Laine Ketner and Walker Percy* (Jackson, MS: University Press of Mississippi).
SAUSSURE, Ferdinand de.
i.1907–1911. *Course in General Linguistics*, trans. Wade Baskins (New York: Philosophical Library, 1959).
SEBEOK, Thomas A. (9 November 1920–2001 December 21).
1963.   "Book review article of M. Lindauer, *Communication among Social Bees*; W. N. Kellog, *Porpoises and Sonar*; and J. C. Lilly, *Man and Dolphin*", *Language* 39, 448–466.
1971.   "'Semiotic' and Its Congeners", in *Linguistic and Literary Studies in Honor of Archibald Hill, I: General and Theoretical Linguistics*, ed. Mohammed Ali Jazayery, Edgar C. Polomé, and Werner Winter (Lisse, Netherlands: Peter de Ridder Press), 283–295; reprinted in Sebeok 1985: 47–58, and in Deely, Williams and Kruse 1986: 255–263.
1972.   *Perspectives in Zoosemiotics* (The Hague: Mouton).
1972a.   "Problems in the Classification of Signs", in *Studies for Einar Haugen*, ed. Evelyn Scherabon Finchow *et al.* (The Hague: Mouton), 511–521, as reprinted in Sebeok 1985: 71–81.
1974.   "Semiotics: A Survey of the State of the Art", in *Linguistics and Adjacent Arts and Sciences*, Vol. 12 of the *Current Trends in Linguistics* series, ed. by Sebeok (The Hague: Mouton), pp. 211–264. Reprinted in Sebeok 1985: 1–45: page references here are to this reprint.
1974a.   "La dynamique des signes", impromptu remarks and discussion reprinted in Sebeok 1985: 95–110.
1975.   "The Semiotic Web: A Chronicle of Prejudices", *Bulletin of Literary Semiotics* 2, 1–63; reprinted "with essential corrections and additions" in Sebeok 1976: 149–188, to which reprint page numbers in the present monograph are keyed.
1975a.   "Zoosemiotics: At the Intersection of Nature and Culture", in *The Tell-Tale Sign*, ed. T. A. Sebeok (Lisse, the

Netherlands: Peter de Ridder Press), pp. 85-95.

1976.   *Contributions to the Doctrine of Signs* (Indiana University, Bloomington, and The Peter De Ridder Press, Lisse).

1977.   "Zoosemiotic Components of Human Communication", in *How Animals Communicate*, ed. Thomas A. Sebeok (Bloomington: Indiana University Press), Chap. 38, pp. 1055-1077.

1977a. "The Semiotic Self", discussion paper presented at the Werner-Reimers-Stiftung in Germany, and subsequently included as Appendix I in Sebeok 1979/1989: 187–207.

1979.   "Semiosis in Nature and Culture", as reprinted in *The Sign & Its Masters* (=Sources in Semiotics VIII; Lanham, MD: University Press of America, 1989), 3–26.

1984a, June 3. "The Evolution of Communication and the Origin of Language", lecture in the June 1–3 ISISSS '84 Colloquium on "Phylogeny and Ontogeny of Communication Systems". Published under the title "Communication, Language, and Speech. Evolutionary Considerations", in Sebeok 1986: 10–16.

1984b. "Vital Signs", Presidential Address delivered October 12 to the ninth Annual Meeting of the Semiotic Society of America, Bloomington, Indiana, October 11–14; subsequently printed in *The American Journal of Semiotics* 3.3 (1985), 1–27, and reprinted in Sebeok 1986: 59–79.

1984c. "Symptom", Chapter 10 of *New Directions in Linguistics and Semiotics*, ed. James E. Copeland (Houston: Rice University Studies), 212–230.

1985.   *Contributions to the Doctrine of Signs* (=Sources in Semiotics IV; reprint of 1976 original with an extended Preface by Brooke Williams, "Challenging Signs at the Crossroads" [Williams 1985], evaluating the book in light of major reviews; Lanham, MD: University Press of America).

1986.   *I Think I Am A Verb. More Contributions to the Doctrine of Signs* (New York: Plenum Press).

1986a. "The Doctrine of Signs", in Deely, Williams and Kruse 1986: 35–42.

1986b. "A Signifying Man", feature review of *Tractatus de Signis* in *The New York Times Book Review* for Easter Sunday, 30 March 1986, pp. 14-15; German translation by Jeff Bernard appears in *Semiotische Berichte* Jg. 11 2/1987: 234-239, with translator's "Anmerkung" p. 240.

1987.   "Language: How Primary a Modeling System?", in *Semiotics 1987*, ed. John Deely (Lanham, MD: University Press of America, 1988), 15–27.

1988.   "In What Sense Is Language a Primary Modeling System?", *Proceedings of the 25th Symposium of the Tartu-Moscow School of Semiotics*, ed. Henri Broms and Rebecca Kaufmann (Helsinki: Artor Inc.), 67–80.

1988a. "In What Sense Is Language a Primary Modeling System?", in *World Behind Words*, ed. F. Steurs. (Leuven: Leuven University Press).

1988b. "Foreword" to the Paperback Edition of Daniel P. Lucid, *Soviet Semiotics: An Anthology* (hardcover ed. 1977; Baltimore: The Johns Hopkins University Press), v–viii.

1988c. "The Notion of 'Semiotic Self' Revisited", in *Semiotics 1988*, ed. Terry Prewitt, John Deely, and Karen Haworth (Lanham: University Press of America, 1989), 189–195.

1989.   *The Sign & Its Masters* (= Sources in Semiotics VIII, ed. John Deely and Brooke Williams; Lanham, MD: University Press of America). Corrected reprint with a new author's Preface (Deely 1989a) of the original imprint of same title (Austin, TX: University of Texas Press 1979).

1989a. "In What Sense Is Language a Primary Modeling System?", in *Worlds Behind Words: Essays in Honour of Prof. Dr. F.G. Droste on the Occasion of His Sixtieth Birthday*, eds. F. J. Heyvaert and F. Steurs (Leuven: Leuven University Press), 25–36.

1989b. "Preface" to *Semiotics, Self, and Society*, ed. Benjamin Lee and Greg Urban (Berlin: Mouton de GruyterLanham: University Press of America, 1989), v.

1990.   "The Sign Science and the Life Science", Address of October 1 to the Hungarian Academy of Sciences, in *"Symbolicity"*, ed. Jeff Bernard, John Deely, Vilmos Voigt, and Gloria Withalm (Papers from the International Semioticians' Conference in Honor of Thomas A. Sebeok's 70th Birthday; Lanham, MD: University Press of America, 1993), 243–252. This volume is bound together with *Semiotics 1990*, ed. Karen Haworth, John Deely, and Terry Prewitt.

1991.   *Semiotics in the United States* (Bloomington, IN: Indiana University Press).

1991a. "In What Sense Is Language a Primary Modeling System?", in *On Semiotic Modeling*, ed. Myrdene Anderson and Floyd Merrell (Berlin: Mouton de Gruyter), 327–339.

1991b. "In What Sense Is Language a Primary Modeling System?" published in Spanish translation, *AdVersuS. Revista de Semiótica* (August).

1998.   "The Estonian connection", *Sign Systems Studies* 26 (1998):

20–41. See http://www.ut.ee/SOSE/sebeok.htm

2001.   *Global Semiotics* (Bloomington, IN: Indiana University Press).

SEBEOK, Thomas A., Editor.

1968.   *Animal Communication: Techniques of Study and Results of Research* (Bloomington, IN: Indiana University Press).

1976.   *A Perfusion of Signs. Transactions of the First North American Semiotics Colloquium, University of South Florida, Tampa, 28–30 July 1975* (Bloomington, IN: Indiana University Press).

SEBEOK, Thomas A., General Editor; Paul BOUISSAC, Umberto ECO, Jerzy PELC, Roland POSNER, Alain REY, Ann SHUKMAN, Editorial Board.

1986.   *Encyclopedic Dictionary of Semiotics* (Berlin: Mouton de Gruyter), in 3 Volumes.

SEBEOK, Thomas A., and Marcel DANESI.

2000.   *The Forms of Meaning.Modeling Systems Theory and Semiotic Analysis* (= Approaches to Applied Semiotics 1; Berlin: Mouton de Gruyter).

SEBEOK, Thomas A., and Susan PETRILLI.

1998.   "Women in Semiotics", in *Interdigitations: Essays for Irmengard Rauch*, ed. Gerald F. Carr, Wayne Harbert, and Lihua Zhang (New York: Peter Lang), 469–478. This essay is included as Chapter 13 in his last book, Sebeok 2001: 145–153.

SEBEOK, Thomas A., and Robert ROSENTHAL, Editors.

1981.   *The Clever Hans Phenomenon: Communication with Horses, Whales, Apes, and People* (New York: The New York Academy of Sciences).

SERRA, Cecilia .

2005?   Syllabus, Inst. de Ling. UniL *Introduction à la Linguistique Générale* 2005-06 Cours n°8.

TARASTI, Eero.

2000.   *Existential Semiotics* (Bloomington, IN: Indiana University Press).

TAYLOR, Daniel.

2008.   "Semiotics & Other Assorted Stories", term paper for Spring 2008 'Philosophy of Knowledge' class at University of St Thomas, Houston, 8 pp.

TRABANT, Jürgen (25 October 1942–).

2004.   *Vico's New Science of Ancient Signs: A Study of Sematology*, trans. from German by Sean Ward (London: Routledge).

VERNADSKY, Vladimir Ivanovich (12 March 1863–1945 January 6).

1926.   The Biosphere, trans. from Russian by D. B. Langmuir (complete annotated ed.; New York: Springer, 1998).

VOIGT, Vilmos.
    1995. "In memoriam of 'Lotmanosphere'," *Semiotica* 105, 191–206.
VON UEXKÜLL, Jakob (8 September 1864–1944 July 25).
    1899–1940. *Kompositionslehre der Natur. Biologie als undogmatische Naturwissenschaft*, selected writings edited and with an introduction by T. von Uexküll (Frankfurt a. M.: Ullstein).
WATT, W. C.
    1978. "Review" of Eco 1976 and Sebeok 1976 (q.v.), *American Anthropologist* 80.3, 714–716.
    2009. "Birth of a Notion", in Cobley, Deely, Kull, and Petrilli, Editors 2009.
WILLIAMS, Brooke (17 August 1941–).
    1982. "The Historian as Observer", in *Semiotics 1982*, ed. John Deely and Jonathan Evans (Lanham, MD: University Press of America, 1987), 13–25.
    1983. "History as a Semiotic Anomaly", in *Semiotics 1983*, ed. Jonathan Evans and John Deely (Lanham, MD: University Press of America, 1987), 409–419.
    1985. "Challenging Signs at the Crossroads", prefatory essay to Sebeok 1976/1985: xv–xlii.
    1985a. *History and Semiotic* (Toronto Semiotic Circle Monograph, No. 4; Victoria University of the University of Toronto).
    1985b. "What Has History To Do with Semiotic", *Semiotica* 54.3/4, 267–333.
    1986. "History in Relation to Semiotic", in Deely, Williams, and Kruse 1986: 217–223.
    1987. "Opening Dialogue between the Discipline of History and Semiotic", in *The Semiotic Web*, ed. Thomas A. Sebeok and Jean Umiker-Sebeok (Berlin: Mouton de Gruyter, 1998), pp. 821–834.
    1987a. "Historiography as a Current Event", in *Semiotics 1987*, ed. John Deely (Lanham, MD: University Press of America).
    1990. "Uma década de debates: História e Semiótica nos annos 80", *Face* 3.1 (janeiro/junho), 11–28.
    1991. "History and Semiotics in the 1990s", *Semiotica* 83.3/4, 385–417.
    2009. "Thomas Sebeok and John Deely on Time", in *Semiotics 2009*, ed. Karen Haworth (Proceedings of the 34th Annual Meeting of the Semiotic Society of America; Ottawa, Canada: Legas), in press.
    2010. "Thomas A. Sebeok: On Semiotics of *History* and History of *Semiotics*", Essay 20 in *Semiotics Continues to Astonish ... How Thomas A. Sebeok shaped the future of the doctrine of*

signs, ed. Paul Cobley, John Deely, Kalevi Kull, and Susan Petrilli (Berlin: Mouton de Gruyter).

2011?   Williams' anthology in the "Semiotics, Communication and Cognition" series (SCC) under the general editorship of Paul Cobley with Kalevi Kull.

ZHAO CHENG & TIAN FAN (Xinhua News Agency), and WEI DONGZE (People's Daily).

2009.   24 December. "Verdant Mountains Cannot Stop Water Flowing; Eastward the River Keeps on Going: Premier Wen Jiabao at the Copenhagen Climate Change Conference", at <http://www.fmprc.gov.cn/eng/zxxx/t648096.htm>.

INDEX

— Greek Terms —

σημεία. 65, 66, 74, 76, 80
σημείον. 61, 65, 74, 77, 82
ημειωτική. 103
σύμβολον. 70, 82

— A —

abduction 88, 114
abductive 55
abstraction 14, 64
Academy 33, 51, 84, 99, 105, 117, 119
accident 79
action of signs 7, 15, 17, 29, 31-36, 38-
  41, 45-48, 52-54, 69, 80, 83, 84, 88,
  89, 91, 93, 96, 107
  See also semiosis *(synonym)*
adaptation 63, 96
aesthetic 48
ages of understanding 15, 104
Albert the Great 59
The American Journal of Semiotics
  99, 101, 103-105, 112, 114, 116
analogical 79
analogy 37, 79
analysis 11, 20, 21, 26, 31, 35, 37, 40,
  43, 55, 67, 71, 78, 95, 118
Analytic philosophy 81
Anderson, Myrdene 18, 38, 93, 99,
  118
animal rationale 13
  See esp. semiotic animal
anthropocentric 44
anthroposemiosis 7, 29, 30, 49, 63, 79,
  90, 104
anthroposemiotic 28, 36, 44
anthroposemiotics 28, 36
anticipation 85
Apology 114
Aquinas, Thomas 39, 43, 44, 47, 52,
  59
arbitrariness 13, 14, 23, 27, 40, 65, 66,
  71, 72, 80, 81
arbitrary 18, 20, 27, 40, 41, 45, 62, 65,
  66, 68, 69, 71, 72, 73
argument 33, 34, 51, 64, 80
Arian 30, 33, 78, 117

Aristotelian 81, 83
Aristotle 42, 43, 46, 53, 55, 56, 58-60,
  74-78, 81-83, 85, 86, 99, 101, 102,
  111
Ashley, Benedict 38, 84, 99
Augustine 17, 18, 31, 39, 44, 74, 79,
  81, 85, 105-107
Australia 50
awareness 13, 17, 23, 44, 53, 57, 60,
  69-72, 75, 78, 96
axiology 48
a-priori 20, 66

— B —

Baer, Eugen 61, 99
Bakhtin, Mikhail 49n66
Bally, Charles 45
Barbieri, Marcello 37n37, 99, 101
  See also biosemiology
Bari, Italy 49, 77, 78, 106
Barthes, Roland 25, 99, 101
Baskin, Wade 70
Baur, Michael 107
Bentham, Jeremy 37, 38
Berger, Asa 105, 114
Bergson, Henri 13, 99
Berkeley, Bishop George 37
Berlin 38, 99, 101, 103, 106, 112, 114,
  117-120
Bernard, Jeff 105, 114, 117, 118
Beuchot, Mauricio 17, 20, 43, 100, 102
Bible 68
biology 32, 33, 36, 72, 83, 95, 105, 110
biosemiology, 36
biosemiotic 27, 30-33, 35, 36, 39, 45,
  95, 96, 99, 101, 103, 110
biosemiotics 27, 31-33, 36, 39, 45, 96,
  103, 110
biosphere 63, 79, 95
Blunden, Andy 86n
Boethius 53, 74, 100
Bonfantini, Massimo A. 49n66
books 49, 59, 83, 99, 114
Bouissac, Paul 38, 39, 83, 100, 108,
  118
"boundary of time" 16

123